171 ADHD Life Hacks
3 Book Series
Impulsivity, Procrastinating, and Time Blindness

Kristen Thrasher

© **Copyright Kristen Thrasher 2023 - All rights reserved.**

The content contained within this book may not be reproduced, duplicated or transmitted without direct written permission from the author or the publisher. Under no circumstances will any blame or legal responsibility be held against the publisher, or author, for any damages, reparation, or monetary loss due to the information contained within this book. Either directly or indirectly. You are responsible for your own choices, actions, and results.

Legal Notice:

This book is copyright protected. This book is only for personal use. You cannot amend, distribute, sell, use, quote or paraphrase any part, or the content within this book, without the consent of the author or publisher.

Disclaimer Notice:

Please note the information contained within this document is for educational and entertainment purposes only. All effort has been executed to present accurate, up-to-date, and reliable, complete information. No warranties of any kind are declared or implied. Readers acknowledge that the author is not engaging in the rendering of legal, financial, medical, or professional advice. The content within this book has been derived from various sources. Please consult a licensed professional before attempting any techniques outlined in this book.

By reading this document, the reader agrees that under no circumstances is the author responsible for any losses, direct or indirect, which are incurred as a result of the use of the information contained within this document, including, but not limited to, — errors, omissions, or inaccuracies.

Other Books by Kristen Thrasher

ADHD Series:
1. Moms With ADHD: Strategies for Women Parenting With Adult ADHD
2. 87 Tips and Tricks for Women With ADHD: Survive the Chaos of Living With Adult ADHD, Manage Your Symptoms, and Live Your Best Life
3. 301 Positive Affirmations for Adults Suffering With ADHD: For Women, Men, and Teens: Learn to Manage Your Impulsiveness, Hyperactivity, Irritability, Time Management, Disorganization, and More
4. ADHD in Adults: 2 Part Series: 87 Tips and Tricks for Women With ADHD and 301 Positive Affirmations for Adults Suffering With ADHD
5. Understanding ADHD in Women: Strategies for Women Diagnosed With ADHD in Adulthood: Manage Your Symptoms as An Adult Living With Attention Deficit Hyperactivity Disorder
6. How ADHD Affects Relationships
7. Relationship Series: Gaslighting in Relationships and How ADHD Affects Relationships
8. ADHD Time Blindness: 27 Hacks to Combat Time Blindness
9. Stop Procrastinating: 47 Hacks to Get Your Ass in Gear
10. Impulsive ADHD: 97 Hacks to Manage Impulsiveness

Eating Disorder Series:
1. Eating Disorders in Children and Teens: A Comprehensive Parent's Guide to Eating Disorder Recovery

2. Understanding Body Dysmorphic Disorder: Causes, Treatment, Self-Care Tips, and Supporting Your Loved One

Gaslighting and Narcissism Series:
1. Gaslighting in Relationships: Why Adults With ADHD are More Vulnerable to Gaslighting Specific Steps to Free Yourself From a Gaslit Relationship
2. Gaslighting Abuse: 66 Tips to Stop a Gaslighter, Including the Gray Rock Method
3. Co-Parenting With a Narcissistic Ex: Strategies For Parallel Parenting When Your Toxic Ex Has Narcissism
4. Narcissistic Relationships: Strategies to Emotionally Detach, Steps to End the Relationship, and Coping Mechanisms to Help You Stay Away
5. Gaslighting and Narcissism 4 Book Series: Gaslighting in Relationships, Gaslighting Abuse, Narcissistic Relationships, and Co-Parenting With a Narcissistic Ex
6. 75 Co-Parenting Hacks: Strategies to Co-Parent With a Narcissist, Improve Your Relationship With Your Ex, Overcome Conflict, and Better Yourself

Parenting Series:
1. Parenting the ADHD Child: 113 Tips and Tricks for Raising a Child With ADHD
2. Parenting the SPD Child: Strategies for Raising a Child With Sensory Processing Disorder
3. Parenting the Autistic Child: 161 Tips and Tricks for Raising a Child on the Autism Spectrum

4. Parenting the Special Needs Child: 124 Tips and Tricks for Parenting a Child With a Disability
5. 4 Book Parenting Series: Parenting the SPD Child, Parenting the ADHD Child, Parenting the Autistic Child, and Parenting the Special Needs Child

Positive Affirmations Series:
1. 409 Positive Affirmations for Recovering From an Eating Disorder
2. 365 Positive Affirmations While Facing a Divorce
3. Positive Affirmations: 3 Book Series Including Divorce, Eating Disorders, and ADHD
4. Positive Self-Love Affirmations

Animal Trivia for Kids Series
1. Horse Trivia: Fun Facts About Horses for Kids
2. Dolphin Trivia: Fun Facts About Dolphins for Kids
3. Animal Trivia for Kids Part 1: Horses and Dolphins
4. Cat Trivia: Fun Facts About Cats for Kids
5. Dog Trivia: Fun Facts About Dogs for Kids
6. Ape and Monkey Trivia: Fun Facts About Apes and Monkeys for Kids
7. Alligator and Crocodile Trivia: Fun Facts About Apes and Monkeys and Alligators and Crocodiles for Kids

Stand-Alone Titles:
1. The Unofficial Friends TV Show Book: The One With all the Quotes

2. Bipolar Disorder Hacks: 47 Tips and Tricks, Self-Management Strategies, and Ways to Cope

**Impulsive ADHD
97 Hacks to Manage Impulsiveness**

Kristen Thrasher

Table of Contents

Introduction
Chapter 1: 37 Daily Hacks to Maximize Your Strengths
Chapter 2: 13 Hacks to Manage Impulsivity
Chapter 3: 19 Self-Help Hacks to Improve Impulsivity
Chapter 4: 23 Hacks to Improve Impulsive Spending
Chapter 5: 5 Hacks to Control Impulsive ADHD
Conclusion

Introduction: Managing Impulsive ADHD

Do you find yourself making decisions without thinking them through? Do you have a difficult time resisting temptation?

Do you find it a little too easy to put another 20 bucks in the slot machine after you've already lost what you promised yourself would be the most you would lose gambling?

Do you find it hard to say no to a second or third drink after you promised yourself you'd only have one when you're out with friends – and they exert the slightest pressure?

Is there even a second thought about staying in bed and calling in sick when you stayed up too late binge-watching your favorite TV show and you're exhausted come morning?

If yes, then you may be struggling with impulsiveness. Impulsivity is a common symptom of ADHD that can make even daily life extremely challenging.

Impulsive ADHD is defined as a pattern of behavior that is characterized by chronic problems with impulsivity. According to the National Institute of Mental Health, people with impulsive ADHD have trouble waiting their turn, acting without thinking, and interrupting others. They also typically have difficulty controlling their emotions and sustaining their attention.

While impulsivity is considered a normal part of childhood development, it is likely time to seek professional help when it begins to interfere with your daily functioning or relationships. Due to their lack of premeditation and their dopamine-seeking behavior, people with ADHD are normally more impulsive than neurotypical people. Even though impulsivity is a common symptom of ADHD, it is not always an indicator of the disorder.

While it can be difficult to diagnose impulsivity on its own (since it can also be a symptom of other conditions like anxiety and bipolar disorder), as many as 60% of people with ADHD will also have impulsivity issues.

Some common examples of impulsive behaviors for adults with ADHD include:

- Lack of self-control at checkout counters, including buying everything in sight
- Struggling to stay on an important task after being suddenly struck with a brilliant idea
- Making big, sometimes even life-changing, decisions without thinking them through
- Blurting out inappropriate, ill-timed, or even hurtful things in conversation

Some impulsive choices might include things such as risky sexual behaviors, overspending, substance abuse, or overindulging with food and drinks.

Many people assume those with impulsive ADHD are simply being rude or chaotic. However, the truth is that people with impulsivity do not have a moral failing or lack of caring. Rather, impulsivity is caused by differences in your brain. Let's take a look at the neuroscience behind impulsive ADHD.

The prefrontal cortex (PFC) is the *driver* of your mind. The PFC regulates decision-making, motivation, and emotions. Abnormal PFC function is associated with ADHD symptoms.

Another brain region involved with impulsivity is the thalamus, known as the *crossing guard.* The thalamus signals the PFC to stop certain behaviors through the dopaminergic pathways. However, this communication is slowed for ADHD brains, which then leads to increased impulsivity.

In layman's terms, the signals that tell non-impulsive neurotypicals to make careful decisions, evaluate, or stop, do not work in ADHD brains quickly enough.

There is not currently an official cause of impulsive ADHD. but research does suggest it is likely caused by a combination of environmental and genetic factors. There is also evidence to suggest that impulsive ADHD runs in families, meaning you are more likely to develop impulsive ADHD if someone in your family has it.

Even though we do not know the exact cause of impulsive ADHD, specific risk factors have been identified, including:

- Maternal smoking, drug use, or alcohol use during pregnancy
- Brain injury
- Low birth weight
- Exposure to toxins, such as lead

Just because you have one or more of these risk factors does not necessarily mean that you will develop impulsive ADHD. In fact, most people who have these risk factors do not develop the disorder. Not having these risk factors doesn't get you off the hook, though. You can have impulsive ADHD without any of them.

If you struggle with impulse control, please understand that you are not alone!

There is no single *quick fix* that will magically turn you into a careful, calculated decision-maker overnight. But you can build new skills that will help you manage your impulsivity with the proper support and practice.

There are several treatment options available for those with impulsive ADHD, including mindfulness practices, medication, psychotherapy, and support groups. Because ADHD treatment looks different for every individual, you should first talk to a mental health professional to create a personalized treatment plan that will work best for you,

Then, you can combine the hacks listed in the chapters ahead alongside your treatment plan. Remember, the hacks are meant to be used in conjunction with your treatment plan, and not in place of it.

In this book, we are going to begin chapter 1 by looking at 37 daily hacks to maximize your strengths. In chapter 2, we look at 13 hacks to manage impulsivity. Then, in chapter 3, we talk about 19 self-help hacks to improve impulsivity. Next, in chapter 4, we jump into 23 hacks to reduce impulsive spending behaviors. Finally, we finish up chapter 5 with 5 hacks to control impulsive ADHD.

We have a long ride ahead of us. It is going to be lots of fun, though! This book is a quick read and shouldn't take you much longer than an hour to make it all the way through. Grab your favorite pen or highlighter so you can take notes. Make yourself a big cup of your favorite comfort drink like coffee or tea. Go get in your comfy spot and cuddle up with your cozy blanket. Now – let's get started.

Chapter 1: 37 Daily Hacks to Maximize Your Strengths

If you have ADHD, you are certainly *not* alone. ADHD is much more common than you may realize. There are several celebrities who have ADHD, including Justin Timberlake, Ryan Gosling, Michael Phelps, Ty Pennington, Adam Levine, and Paris Hilton.

There can be many wonderful, amazing traits that you possess because you have ADHD, including:

- You are highly creative.
- You tend to be extremely caring and empathetic.
- You find joy in even the smallest of pleasures.
- You have above-average intelligence.
- You tend to think "outside of the box".
- You have unique solutions to problems.

The list *truly* goes on and on. But with all of the beautiful traits that people with ADHD have, there also comes a list of challenges.

You want to be able to face your challenges head on in order for your amazing qualities to be able to shine through. In this chapter, we are going to look at 37 different life hacks you can use on a *daily* basis to improve yourself. The fact that the hacks in this chapter are short and sweet does not make them any less important – or effective.

I want to personally challenge you to try at least five of these hacks starting today. Choose any five hacks. Do each hack, consistently, every day for at least seven days. Then, see how you feel. You can stop if you didn't notice any improvement. But, I'm willing to bet that will not be the case.

1. **Reward yourself.**

    Create rewards for yourself as you accomplish your tasks. Make sure you have a bigger reward for the bigger project or task you complete. A reward doesn't have to be something monetary. It could be allowing yourself to watch your favorite movie or go for a walk after you finish your project.

2. **Stop trying to multitask.**

    Multitasking does *not* actually do any good - for anyone! While some people are able to multitask, you my friend, are *not*. Multitasking is your greatest enemy. That is a-okay. Don't even attempt to multitask. Ever. It is not worth it. Focus on one thing at a time. When you finish what you are working on, move on to the next thing. It's that simple. Otherwise, you will struggle to finish anything.

3. **Calm down when you begin to feel stressed or emotional.**

Don't ever start working on a new project when you are feeling emotional or stressed. This rule especially applies when you are sad. Always wait to work on the project until you are in the right mindframe.

4. **Keep your things organized.**

    Get an organizer you can divide into small, separate compartments. This could even be something as simple as a little basket. Label each separate compartment with the different categories required to organize your most important items. This will help remind you to put everything in its "home" when you are done.

5. **Harness the power of hyperfocus.**

    It is perfectly normal to allow yourself to be completely swept away sometimes. Don't even stop to take a break when you become totally immersed in a project and are actually accomplishing something. There are many times when being *in the zone* is an excellent thing.

6. **Use your voice to commit important things to memory.**

    When you find yourself without pen and paper after receiving important instructions or verbal information, repeat what was said out loud to yourself three to four times. Then, immediately go and find somewhere to write it down. You can even text it to yourself! Repeating the information out loud will allow you to remember what was said until you are able to put it onto paper.

7. **Don't clutter your study/work space.**

Some people are able to work well amid clutter. You are not one of them. It just won't work. Don't blame yourself, it's the ADHD. Because you know this ahead of time, you should always keep your study or work space as orderly and uncluttered as possible.

8. **Keep a to-do list printed out in front of you.**

You need to have a visual to-do list right in front of you at all times in order to keep your focus sharp. And I do mean *literally* right in front of you. This does not mean in the back of your day planner or in a file on your laptop. You will be more motivated to get more accomplished when you are readily able to see your to-do list at all times.

9. **Always hold onto your to-do list.**

If you throw away your to-do list before you have completed the entire list, you may forget something important. Don't ever throw it away until you have crossed every single item off. If you have some items remaining, transfer them to a new list before discarding the prior one.

10. **Check your calendar twice a day.**

You can *never* check your calendar enough, because you don't know what you might be forgetting. You should always check it a minimum of twice a day. This includes every morning when you wake up and again every night before you go to bed. This ensures you don't forget anything you should be doing.

11. **Don't try to clean daily.**

    Rather than trying to clean a little every single day, it is smarter to dedicate one day each week for cleaning. You put too much stress on yourself when you try to clean your house everyday. Tip: Make it the same day every week and it will become part of your routine!

12. **Turn the TV off so you won't become distracted.**

    Let's be honest: if the TV is turned on, you *will* become distracted. You will inevitably find yourself watching the TV and lose all track of time. To prevent this, don't even turn on the TV in the morning when you are getting ready for school or work. If you absolutely must be updated on the daily events, you can listen to the radio or a podcast on your way to work instead.

13. **Keep your brain tidy.**

    Write down all of your thoughts on a piece of paper as you become distracted by them when you are trying to focus on school or work projects. You will be better able to remain focused when you release these thoughts in writing and clear your mind of all clutter.

14. **When you can, go with the flow.**

When there's something specific on TV you want to watch, go ahead and take a break from doing the dishes. You deserve a break, just like everyone else does. When you are not in the middle of doing something urgent, it is perfectly normal to let yourself get distracted. Just make sure not to make this a habit, or to let yourself get distracted when you are in the middle of something important. Remember, *moderation in everything.*

15. **Choose only one place for your stuff.**

Because you have ADHD, you will be prone to misplacing your things. You will be much less likely to lose your things when you keep all of your important items in one place. Choose a special spot both at home and at work. Items to consider include your purse, wallet, keys, and phone.

16. **Pause before speaking.**

People with ADHD are known for blurting things out, often inappropriately. Pause to repeat or paraphrase what was said to you as you are listening to someone else before vocalizing your response. You can even repeat exactly what they said back to them out loud. This gives you several seconds to mull over your response, and will also clarify any potential misconceptions. You could also come up with a secret signal to give yourself before saying something out loud in a meeting or class. This will remind you to stop and think before you blurt out something that you will likely regret later. For example, this could be something as simple as putting your finger to your lips.

17. Laughter is a great thing.

You have heard it said that *laughter is the best medicine*, right? It's true! You can find humor in anything if you put your mind to it. So, why not find humor in your ADHD, too? Go ahead and make jokes about it! Trust me, this alone will make you feel much better.

18. If you think of something, write it down immediately.

You should always keep a pad of paper or small dry erase board in a specific spot in every room of your house so you can write down important things as they come to you. This ensures you don't forget any brilliant ideas you may have throughout the day. At the end of every day, make sure to consolidate all of these lists. You will be surprised at how many great ideas you had during the day!

19. Don't try to work too long at a time.

Everyone needs breaks, especially people with ADHD. Make sure that you are taking frequent breaks. Try to do some movement during these breaks. It is exciting to look forward to the "ding" of a timer, so go ahead and set an alarm for your break time.

20. Get ahead of yourself.

When you live five to ten minutes ahead of the rest of the world, you are more likely to make it on time even when you become distracted. Set all of your clocks for 5 to 10 minutes ahead of time. Trick: set each of your clocks for a *different* time. This way, you don't know exactly what time it is. All you know is that you are, in fact, ahead of time.

21. **Place important things within easy reach.**

Find a specific place to put everything you need to take with you to school or work the next morning. Every night before you go to bed, put all of your important items in this exact spot. Think of everything you might need in the morning, including keys, purse, wallet, phone, books, files, etc.

22. **Always be prepared to take notes.**

You should always carry a pad of paper with you because you never know when you are going to need to take notes. It really doesn't matter how big or how small your notepad is. You can get a notebook with a pen holder, too.

23. **Count on your loved ones.**

You may be an extremely independent man/woman who feels as if you must do everything by yourself. But your loved ones *want* to help you. So let them! They can do something as small as remind you of when your upcoming appointments are or other things you need to accomplish.

24. **Use technology to pay your bills.**

　　You can easily arrange an automatic payment to come out of your checking account every month. This ensures that you won't miss any deadlines or get your electricity cut off if you forget to pay the bill. This is extra beneficial if you, like me, have a hard time remembering to pay your bills. Because all banks keep a record of everything you have paid, along with the dates of the last payment, it is easy and convenient for you to check for possible cases of fraud.

25. **Isolate yourself when you need to focus.**

　　It is recommended to find a quiet place to isolate yourself when you need to focus. It should have either dark window shades or no windows at all. You can use ear plugs if you are unable to block out all of the noise, or you can even try using "white noise".

26. **Sticky notes are your friend.**

　　Become friends with the sticky note, or post-it note. You will need a plethora of sticky notes at all times. Try putting each of your errands on an individual sticky note and stick them on the dashboard of your car. Then, get rid of the sticky note after you complete the errand. This allows you to easily see what you still need to accomplish for each trip.

27. **Put your cell phone aside when you are busy.**

The best thing you can do sometimes is to simply put down your phone. If you have someone you can trust, let them hold on to it for a while so you can work on your project. Instruct them to only answer calls from family members or emergencies. Silence notifications and go without any interruptions to really see progress!

28. **Have a planner or calendar with you at all times.**

    You absolutely must keep some kind of a day planner or calendar with you at all times. If you prefer to use an app, that is perfectly fine. However, you need to also have a calendar on the wall to serve as a visual aid you are able to see throughout the day. Make sure to transfer all of your specific dates and appointments to your wall calendar.

29. **Color-code to set priorities.**

    Many people use post-it notes on their wall calendars. An easy way to prioritize your tasks is to color-coordinate these post-it notes. For example, red post-it notes could signify your most urgent requests. This system also makes your calendar much prettier, so it's a win-win!

30. **Don't let your active brain cheat you out of sleep.**

    Sometimes we wake up in the middle of the night with the greatest idea in the world. The next time this happens to you, turn on the light. Grab the piece of paper you keep on your nightstand and immediately write down all of your thoughts. Don't let these racing thoughts keep you up all night! You must get them out of your system. But, you can get back to whatever brilliant idea you had in the morning after you wake up. After you get your thoughts written down, turn off the light and go back to sleep!

31. **Pay all of your bills at once.**

Your life will be much easier if you coordinate your bills so you can pay them all at the same time. It is easy to arrange for all of your bills to be due at the same time. This makes it harder for you to forget paying anything each month. All you need to do is contact all of your utilities and creditors to request the same time frame. You will be pleasantly surprised by how many are happy to oblige.

32. **Don't let the Internet become a distraction.**

You must always give yourself a specific amount of time to spend on the Internet so it doesn't become a distraction you are unable to walk away from. Set a timer to control your schedule.

33. **Purge.**

As soon as you finish a project, take all of the paperwork you were using and *throw it away immediately!* You don't need it. Don't hoard it. Get rid of everything you have no use for anymore. There is absolutely no need to hang on to all of your past projects you don't need any longer.

34. **Have a medication back up plan.**

    You should always keep a small backup supply of your meds in your purse or even your desk at work. You never know when you will forget to take your medication at home. Trust me, you will be happy you remembered and had the foresight to prepare for emergencies.

35. **Divide reading assignments.**

    Rather than attempting to read a long reading assignment or entire book at once, divide it up into smaller sections between now and the due date. Make a schedule for when you will read each section. It helps to put post-it notes on these divisions to show how much you need to read and when. This will allow you to be more productive and also remember and retain what you are reading.

36. **Walk and talk.**

    You have likely seen many people pacing when they are on the phone, especially those with ADHD. Turns out, there is an actual reason for this! Research shows that you remain more focused on what you are talking about when you walk at the same time. Try pacing when you are engaged in important phone conversations and see for yourself the difference it can make!

37. **ADHD does not define you.**

If you don't remember any other hacks, please remember this one: you *have* ADHD; you *are not* ADHD. It is simply one of your many characteristics. Don't ever let ADHD be the defining feature of your personality. Constantly remind yourself of your strengths and talents when you are feeling down and low. Do this over and over until you start believing how important you are!

Having ADHD can be both a curse and a blessing. Yes, you are antsy. Yes, you probably have difficulty focusing in order to complete tasks. And, yes, you can be self-destructive and impulsive.

However, you are also a strong individual whose brain is in *rapid fire* mode a lot more frequently than neurotypical people. This mode is what allows you to solve problems creatively.

The hacks you just learned in this chapter are going to help you minimize your *curses* while simultaneously maximizing your *blessings*.

Chapter 2: 13 Hacks to Manage Impulsivity

People with impulsive ADHD are prone to act before taking the time to think. They are also quick to say things they don't mean, interrupt others, and make commitments they cannot keep. Impulsive people often put themselves in risky situations without realizing it and overindulge in things like intoxicating substances, sex, eating, or shopping,

Do any of the above descriptions ring a bell? While everyone struggles with impulsiveness occasionally, it is a *constant* battle for those with impulsive ADHD.

Even though impulsivity is rarely easy to overcome, it *can* be managed effectively with the right tools and amount of effort. The 13 hacks listed in this chapter will help you identify your triggers and learn to manage your ADHD-related impulsivity.

1. Create a gap between impulse and action.

It is difficult for people with ADHD to pause or slow down. This is why it is so helpful to find alternative activities to fill the gap between impulse and action. Oftentimes, even a few moments of careful consideration can be enough to stop an impulse.

Force yourself to take a deep breath when you feel your impulses starting to take over, especially when you are in the habit of agreeing too quickly to requests or interrupting others. You can practice using some various filler phrases to buy some extra time, such as "That's an interesting idea" or "I will have to think about that." You can also repeat what the person said back to them while considering your response. Another suggestion is to carry a bottle of water around with you. Take a drink whenever you get the impulse to speak too quickly.

Whichever trick you use, always take the time to think things through before speaking or acting them out. The more of a delay you create, the better off you will be.

2. **Learn emotional management skills.**

Because strong emotions make it harder to inhibit yourself from immediately acting on a thought, you are much more likely to say something hurtful when you are angry. There are several emotional management skills you can learn to regulate your emotions more effectively including self-care, mindfulness practices, and exercise Mindfulness is extremely effective as it enables self-monitoring while simultaneously calming you down. Find a specific mindfulness strategy that works best for you, and do it as often as possible. Some examples include meditation, guided imagery, breathing exercises, and grounding techniques.

3. **Remove triggers.**

   Triggers can be either situational or emotional. For example, you may have the impulse to criticize friends or co-workers when they point out your mistakes. In order to remove this trigger, bear in mind that they are on your side and trying to help you.

   Triggers can also be physical. Many people with ADHD suffer impulses surrounding eating. For example, if it is too hard for you to have only one potato chip without eating the entire bag, then remove the trigger by not keeping chips in your house. Make a rule to allow yourself only one snack-sized bag of chips every week. And if you must keep chips in the house, make sure to store the bag at the back of the pantry so you will not see your biggest temptation every time you open the door.

4. **Be spontaneous, not impulsive.**

   About two seconds of thought separate spontaneous and impulsive behaviors. You are more likely to process the pros and cons of your situation when you slow down, even briefly, to allow yourself an informed decision before you act. You don't necessarily need to reduce your *fun* in order to reduce your *impulsivity.* However, acting spontaneously instead of impulsively will typically end in fewer negative consequences.

5. **Keep the right company.**

Consider the influence your peers have over you and be strategic about who comes along for potentially triggering activities. There is no reason to cut people out of your life when they add value to it. However, if seeing your Facebook friend's posts tempt you to quickly reply with a sarcastic comment, adjust your app settings so you no longer see that person's posts anymore. Likewise, if your best friend is an impulsive shopper, her behavior might, unfortunately, rub off on you. Avoid being with another impulsive person regardless of how much fun you have shopping with her.

6. **Wear an elastic band.**

    Keep an elastic band around your wrist and snap the band as soon as you feel the urge to act impulsively. This technique will bring you to your senses and jar you back to the present moment, that, in turn, can help you break unhelpful patterns that cause you to act impulsively.

7. **Imagine the future.**

    You can make a pretty accurate assumption of the *future* by thinking back to your impulsive moments in your *past*. When you feel the impulse to say or do something, first stop and ask yourself if it will be healthy or safe. Try to imagine how good you will feel if you react thoughtfully (confident and competent), rather than acting on your impulse (shameful and regretful). Think of ways you can improve the consequence. For example, if openly criticizing your boss's idea did not work out well for you in the past, it's not likely to work out well for you in the future either. You can also use this technique by using visual reminders. For example, if you are trying to save for a big vacation but know you struggle with online shopping, tape a picture of your destination to your laptop screen so you will see it each time you start to shop online and be reminded of what you are saving money for.

8. **Identify weak spots.**

    You will have your own unique weak spots depending on your personality type. Picture the specific ways and environments in which you typically lose your inhibitions. Make a list of past situations in which you were impulsive to properly identify your weak spots by naming which were the most problematic. For example, if impulsive eating is a weak spot for you, ask yourself where you are the majority of the time you overindulge. Are you at work? At home? At a restaurant? What specific things happen right before you take the first bite? Does someone offer you something? Or do you feel stressed, lonely, or bored? All of these facts will help you formulate a plan to avoid being impulsive in the future.

9. **Avoid your weaknesses.**

    Brainstorm specific things you can do to avoid your most troublesome weak spots. You can use the hacks listed in this chapter to devise a plan for each one and add it to your triggers list. If one hack isn't working, try implementing it differently or try a new hack altogether. Treat your contingency plans as a work in progress so that you revisit them often. Don't limit yourself to the hacks listed in this book: get creative and develop some of your own coping mechanisms. You can also visit online forums to learn from other people's experiences with impulsive ADHD.

10. **Create obstacles.**

    Create obstacles for yourself by setting up barriers between you and your impulsive behaviors. Leave yourself physical reminders that force you to pause before acting on your impulses. For example, try writing on a sticky note, "I only drink on the weekend so I don't feel hungover at work." Then place this note on your liquor cabinet so you must read it before you can even get to the alcohol inside. Or, take a responsible friend with you to the bar so you are not tempted to bring a stranger home with you. Use your imagination; there are a wide variety of obstacles you can create to avoid impulsive behavior.

11. **Consider professional support.**

    People who don't know what it's like to have impulsive ADHD may assume you are being intentionally rude because they do not realize how hard you are trying to control your impulses. They will probably not be very understanding or supportive. This is why it is so important for you to work with a therapist who specializes in adult ADHD. A therapist can help accelerate your progress in overcoming impulsive behaviors by providing unbiased perspective, evidence-based strategies, and consistent support. A licensed therapist can also refer you to a prescribing physician if you wish to inquire about medication as another form of treatment.

12. **Know yourself.**

　　　　Knowing yourself means learning which things, places, and people push your buttons and understanding the role you play in allowing those buttons to be pushed. In other words, knowing yourself means learning your impulsivity triggers. Some examples of questions to ask yourself include: *Which situations make you more likely to make impulsive decisions? Does doing drugs or drinking alcohol increase your impulsivity? Does shopping cause you to spend money you don't have? Do you tend to overeat when you are alone and emotional?* See which triggers can be minimized, and which triggers you are able to remove yourself from completely. It is absolutely crucial that you avoid your specific triggers at all costs. *Prevention* is always better than *damage control.*

13. **Make a phone call.**

Often, when an impulse strikes, the passage of time can keep you from acting in a way you might later regret. Think of it as a cooling off period, a period of time wherein you can come to your senses and realize that your impulse is just that - an impulse - and not a sound idea that serves you well. One way to accomplish this delay is to make a quick phone call to a friend. Find someone you can trust and ask them if you can call them for a pep talk when you are tempted to do something you may later regret. The ten minutes you spend with them may be all you need to change your mood and take you away from the urge you had.

Chapter 3: 19 Self-Help Hacks to Improve Impulsivity

If you're like the majority of people, you began panicking just reading the title of this chapter. *Self-help.* Why does talking about self-help cause you to panic? It should be the very first thing on your list! Rather, it's typically the last. Self-help is *not at all selfish!* You will never be able to take care of those you love if you're not properly taking care of yourself first.

Please don't skip over this chapter. And please don't be afraid or think you are doing anything wrong because it is called *self-help.* I promise, it's okay! The guilt and other emotions you are feeling right now are further proof that you need some self-help. You deserve to take care of yourself, too!

Let's take a look at 19 specific self-help strategies to help you improve your impulsivity.

1. **Exercise.**

    Many people with ADHD are impulsive due to hyperactivity, so exercise is an excellent way to burn off that extra energy. Exercise is a way to treat ADHD naturally because it improves both concentration and focus. Not only does it improve your mood and reduce your stress levels, but it also allows you to burn off excess energy that leads to making impulsive decisions. Even a daily walk is enough to see improvement. Make it your goal to do at least 20 minutes of moderate exercise every day. In order to create a lasting habit, make sure you choose something you enjoy doing.

2. **Be mindful.**

One way to sharpen your self-awareness is to practice mindfulness techniques. Start by bringing your attention to the present moment and observe what is happening without judgment. Focus on your emotions, thoughts, urges, and how your body feels when you begin to feel impulsive. While it won't be easy in the beginning, you will likely pick up on your impulsivities only *after* being impulsive. As with most things, you will be able to start identifying what causes your impulsive behavior with practice. Mindfulness also helps you gain some distance from your urges. For instance, rather than being driven by your impulses, you will now only be observing them from a distance. This enables you to be better equipped to decide your next action. Let's look at some examples of how this might look:

- Practice how to recognize an urge before you act impulsively.
- Put a specific name on that urge, such as "This is anger I am feeling."

- Identify the action that emotion is leading you to, such as "I want to yell at my boss because I am angry."
- Name exactly what you need to do in order to stop the impulsive behavior, such as "I need to step away, take a moment, and come back later when I have calmed down" or "I need to express my frustration without making it personal."
- Wait to approach the situation until your urge has decreased.
- Document your emotion, what you felt like doing in the moment, and then what you actually ended up doing so you can come back later and learn from your actions.

3. **Simplify your hygiene routine.**

    It is imperative that you simplify your hygiene routine when impulsivity is something you struggle with constantly. There is absolutely no reason to have a 25-step skincare routine when you have much more important issues to work on. Use dry shampoo, seek an accountability partner, and be kind to yourself with the many ups and downs you will experience.

4. **Love yourself.**

    Make an effort to practice truly *loving yourself* every single day, day in and day out. One way to start is by writing a positive affirmation on a sticky note then place it somewhere you will see it every day, such as the bathroom mirror. Start with something simple, such as "I am enough." Make sure it is strategically placed so that you will always see it. Regularly switch up your positive affirmation to create subtle inner love and self-hype. You *deserve* to be loved – especially by yourself!

5. **Show yourself compassion.**

    You are human. All you can do is the best you can. It is *okay* to make mistakes. You can't overcome impulsivity overnight, and there is no need to! It takes practice to overcome impulsivity, especially as an adult. Treat setbacks as a learning opportunity instead of getting frustrated with yourself and giving up. Avoid spirals of shame as you make steady progress towards your goals with self-compassion and patience. Use whatever information you gain to plan continued experimentation and future improvements. You can decrease the negative emotions that often exacerbate impulsivity when you practice self-compassion. Remember, *slow and steady wins the race.*

6. **Build boundaries.**

    People *will* take advantage of you if you do not set boundaries for yourself. Boundaries are extremely important for your health and well-being. People with ADHD have a difficult time saying no to requests from others. But, you must give yourself permission to not participate, especially if you accidentally agreed to something without seriously thinking it through first. This is just one thing that will keep you from burning yourself out.

7. **Try yoga.**

    Even 10 to 15 minutes of yoga every day will make a huge difference in your stress levels, frustration tolerance, and well-being. There is no need to practice yoga for hours at a time. No matter what age you are, you can find a place for yoga in your life. It truly has benefits for everyone, young and the old.

8. **Analyze yourself.**

    Try approaching impulsivity as a logical scientist would solve a puzzle. Practice labeling your impulsivity by writing out the situation. Make sure you account for how you felt before you acted and leave notes for what you should do next time in order to stop the impulsive behavior.

9. **Engage in relaxing activities.**

    Impulsive ADHD is only made worse when you are stressed or on edge. You can increase your impulse control by engaging in relaxing activities. Some examples of relaxing activities that help with impulse control include:
    - Practicing guided imagery
    - Implementing deep breathing techniques throughout the day

- Listening to calming music, especially when you need to get busy
- Exercising as often as possible
- Learning progressive muscle relaxation

10. **Get enough protein.**

    Many people have carb-heavy diets, meaning they lack adequate amounts of protein which is necessary for your body to produce neurotransmitters, such as dopamine. You already know that a lack of dopamine is exactly what leads to dopamine-seeking behaviors, such as impulsivity. Consider any way you increase your dopamine levels a win-win!

11. **Increase dopamine naturally.**

    In order to control impulsivity, you need to prevent your dopamine-seeking behavior by acquiring more dopamine in healthy and natural ways. Exercising and simply *having fun* are just a couple healthy ways you can increase your body's dopamine levels.

12. **Inhale essential oils.**

    Another way you can maintain healthy dopamine levels is to include regular essential oil breaks throughout your day. There are several essential oils that are linked to healthy dopamine levels, including Lemon, Lavender, and Bergamot.

13. **Set limits on screen time**

    Research has proven that too much screen time causes ADHD symptoms to worsen by leading to impulsiveness and restlessness. You must be mindful of your time in front of a phone, tablet or monitor in order to ensure that you are spending enough time offline. You can help yourself stay focused and avoid making unnecessary impulsive decisions by setting limits on your screen time.

14. **Schedule your meals.**

It is difficult to break the bad habits of skipping meals and binge eating. You should always try to get a protein-rich shake or meal first thing in the morning because it helps regulate your appetite and ensures your body has what it needs to make things like dopamine.

15. **Adopt a mantra.**

The bad days will inevitably come. Everyone has bad days, everyone. You are not immune to having bad days. Don't for a second believe you will be the exception. No matter how many hacks you put into practice, your impulsive behaviors will still come through on occasion. Adopt a mantra for the bad days when nothing else seems to be working. Start by repeating a specific mantra that has meaning to you. For example, "Now is not here forever; be here now." Or, "This, too, shall pass." Come up with different ideas until you find the perfect mantra just for you.

16. **Indulge when down.**

Everyone needs some rest and relaxation, *all things in moderation.* Treat yourself to the perfect date - with yourself! Give yourself permission to go *all out.* Eat a snack you wouldn't normally eat, put on an expensive face mask, watch your favorite movie, and recline on the couch at the end of a long day. *Take all the time you need.* You must realize this is not at all selfish. In fact, this is *mandatory.*

17. **Use supplements.**

Look for specific supplements, such as high-quality, bioavailable supplements that are derived from whole foods. Deficiencies in omega 3 fatty acids, vitamin D, and zinc can cause impulsivity.

18. **Practice gratitude.**

Try to practice gratitude, and at the same time every day. Set a reminder on your phone. Immediately stop whatever you are doing as soon as the *ding* goes off. Just be *still* and think of one thing you are truly grateful for in that exact moment. Sit and think about that one thing for a full 60 seconds.

19. **Take off your cape.**

Everyone feels like they have to be superheroes at times. And you might be pretty damn close. After all, it is fun and exciting to swoop in and save the day. Just make sure you don't lose yourself along the way. You don't have to be *perfect.* You don't have to take care of everyone around you. It's okay to just *be* sometimes. Try to be realistic in how much you are able to handle. Moderation in everything (that cannot be stressed enough). You must have balance. Repeat after me: *I am human.*

Chapter 4: 23 Hacks to Improve Impulsive Spending

Do you spend impulsively when you find something you like so much that you must have it right *now?* Even though it can be thrilling and exciting in the moment, it may quickly become a concern as you realize your finances are suffering because of your impulsive spending habit.

Impulsive spending is that *spur of the moment* decision to buy something that isn't planned. Because the idea of "acting now and worrying about it later" is so prevalent among people with ADHD, it is common for such impulsive habits to carry over into the world of spending as well.

This brings us back to the link between dopamine and impulsivity. We talked about dopamine, the neurotransmitter that makes you feel happy, fulfilled, and pleasured. You know your brain releases dopamine when you perform an activity that makes you happy or excited.

Because one of the key markers of ADHD is low dopamine levels in the brain, people with ADHD are often on the search for more dopamine, albeit subconsciously, which is known as "dopamine-seeking behavior".

Impulsive spending enhances the feelings of pleasure; it causes more dopamine to be released which, in turn, creates intense motivation to repeat this process over and over. This is exactly why impulsive spending can become such a nasty habit.

Dopamine-seeking behavior can also create an addiction to other impulsive behaviors that provide that dopamine rush. Unfortunately, this rush is often followed by a crash back to reality when the consequences of the behaviors appear. Like the bill at the end of the month!

Many people with impulsive ADHD feel as if they are doomed to impulsive spending habits. However, there are several hacks you can put into practice in order to stop impulsive spending and regain control of your finances.

In this chapter, we are going to look at 23 specific hacks that are geared towards gaining control over *your* impulsive spending habits.

1. **Minimize online shopping.**

    Online shopping makes it extremely convenient to have your items delivered to you without ever leaving your house. It also makes it far too easy to spend large amounts of money in a very short amount of time. You can easily have thousands of dollars worth of extremely unnecessary items on their way to your house in a matter of minutes, with only a few clicks of the mouse. In order to avoid overspending online, only shop in physical stores. However, you must also train yourself to steer clear of any mall that has a chance of distracting you with other shopping opportunities.

2. **Try a month-long "No Spend Challenge".**

    Only allow yourself to buy groceries and other necessities for an entire month during the "No Spend Challenge". *Nothing* else. You will be pleasantly surprised at how much money you will begin to save, especially when you are in the routine of spending impulsively. After you successfully complete one month, you can reward yourself with something small using the money you just saved.

3. **Ask yourself, "Where will this item live?"**

    When you are shopping and feel the sudden urge to buy something, stop and ask yourself, "Where will this item live?" You will likely have a moment of clarity when you stop to visualize your new item's place in your life as you may realize you don't have the space for the item. Therefore, there is no need to purchase the item.

4. **Know why you go shopping.**

    It is always important to know why you are shopping. Some days you shop because you legitimately need something. However, other days you shop because you had a bad day and needed a *special treat.* If it's the latter, there is no reason to even go shopping in the first place! You are much more likely to impulsively spend more than you had planned on when you are in this frame of mind. In fact, I'm sure you have heard of the term "retail therapy"? This is *exactly* where this term came from! Try to come up with other ideas of how to reward yourself after having a bad day at the office.

5. **Unsubscribe to retail emails and texts.**

You will never be tempted to spend impulsively on a bunch of items that you don't need if you didn't receive the marketing. You literally would never even know about the deals if you didn't get the promotion emails or texts. You must unsubscribe from all retail chains so you stop receiving an unlimited supply of emails and texts promoting all of the latest sales. You can also ask to have yourself removed from snail mail lists if your mailbox is clogged with catalogs.

6. **Shop with cash.**

Not only should you only use cash when you shop, but you should also only take the specific amount of cash you are wanting to spend in one shopping trip. This will enable you to only focus on getting what you intended to purchase ahead of time. This also prevents you from being able to reach for your credit cards when you decide impulsively you *have* to have something out of your budget. You are better able to understand exactly how much you are spending when you use cash, which makes it a *right now* problem. It is far too easy to swipe with a card, making it a problem for "future you".

7. **Limit the number of times you visit a store or shop online.**

   Don't ever just browse or "window shop" because this will undoubtedly get you into trouble every single time. Instead, only visit a store, whether in person or online, if you have a specific list of the exact items you intend to purchase on that trip. Better yet, you can avoid shopping online completely if you have a spouse, parent or friend buy things for you. Assuming you have a level of trust with your shopper by proxy, you can let them borrow your PC or laptop to order items, or they can order the item and you can pay them back.

8. **Allow yourself a treat purchase.**

   Give yourself a treat purchase that A) keeps you from feeling deprived of the joy of shopping, and B) allows you to stay within your budget. However, make sure you keep the receipts on your treat purchase so you will be able to return the item if you change your mind.

9. **Calculate the item's value in terms of the hours you have to work for it.**

   It doesn't take you too long to figure out the math. Simply divide the price of the item by how much you make per hour. This gives you the number of hours you must work to pay for this item. Ask yourself: *is this item worth that many hours of your life?*

10. **Use apps to help you track your spending.**

    One of the best ways to limit impulsive spending is to pay attention to your overall spending. You may be prone to impulsively spend in one small area of your life. You will likely try to rationalize it away by telling yourself that you will save somewhere else, but that might be a lie you use as a crutch. You know perfectly well that you don't actually plan on cutting out anything else. Apps are an extremely easy way for beginners to track their expenses. There are many apps that can help you track your spending and see how closely you stick to your budget. Many apps will even allow you to set certain spending limits. The app Rocket Money is the easiest way to find subscriptions, manage bills, and even cancel recurring charges with a single click.

11. **Take someone with you when shopping in person.**

    Always take a close friend or family member shopping with you and tell them what you plan to purchase. This way, they can hold you accountable for all of your purchases. You should also tell your friend or family member immediately when you find yourself itching to shop online.

12. **Delete credit card and other payment information.**

You will be much less tempted to make a purchase online when you are required to fill out your information every single time. So don't ever save your payment information or credit card on file, especially at places you find yourself spending impulsively. You can even go as far as eliminating card information from your virtual wallet. Any extra steps you have to take before purchasing an item gives you extra time to decide whether you really need the item. This also makes it not as convenient to spend impulsively.

13. **Make it a rule to not buy anything in the checkout lane.**

    You have likely been tempted, along with everyone else in the world, to buy items in the checkout lane. Whether it's a hair tie or chapstick, scotch tape or bubble gum, you don't need to buy it if it wasn't on your shopping list.

14. **Wait 24 hours before purchasing.**

    Wait at least 24 hours before purchasing something you really want. Always resist buying whatever you want immediately. It is especially important to wait if it is a *big* purchase. Give yourself some time to answer these questions: *Will this item significantly improve my life? Do I really need it? Is it worth the cost?* Only make the purchase if you can safely answer yes to all three questions. You will eliminate the quick hit of dopamine you get from spending impulsively when you postpone your purchase for at least 24 hours. You may even notice you no longer want the item when you go back to purchase it the next day.

15. **Keep your saving goals in mind with a visual reminder.**

    Place your saving goals in as many places as possible to be constantly reminded that limiting your impulsive spending will be beneficial to you in the long run. For example, you can place your saving goal on your door, the fridge, your phone's lock screen, and even your car's dashboard. Let's say you want to save for a trip to Hawaii. Put a picture of a beautiful island beach somewhere prominent so you remember what you're saving for!

16. **Treat your ADHD.**

    You get a big shot of dopamine when you make any kind of purchase, and because your brain has less dopamine than those without ADHD, that dopamine feels extremely good to you. Everyone likes to do things that make them feel good. Hence, the never-ending cycle of impulsive spending. But, dopamine levels are increased when you are treating your ADHD. In turn, self-medicating behaviors, such as shopping, don't seem quite as compelling when you have no need for the extra dopamine.

17. **Make shopping lists.**

Always plan ahead of time, when you are away from your temptations, what you need to buy. Then create a list. Never go shopping without creating a list first, and don't buy anything that isn't on your shopping list. If you do happen to find something on sale that is not on your list, you can add it to your list for another day. You will be able to remain focused on staying on track with your spending when you include only the items you need on your shopping list.

18. **Only buy returnable items and learn to return.**

    Most impulse purchases will lose your interest rather quickly because you likely didn't need the item in the first place. You are giving yourself the option to literally *fight back* against your own impulses when you ensure you have the option to return the items. Always look for stores who have a return period of up to three months or longer. Consider if you still want the item a week or two after making the purchase. If not, you will easily be able to return it. Never exchange the money for another item. Instead, always make sure to get your money back and immediately place it back into your overall budget.

19. **Keep your receipts.**

    Many people with ADHD are not able to return their items due to losing their receipts. If you follow the previous hack and only purchase items from stores that allow you to return, then you always have the option to return the item as long as you can keep up with your receipts. Create a special place to keep all of your receipts while you are shopping in your purse or wallet. Transfer them to a special envelope or folder when you get home. Keep every single one, even for items you had already planned on buying ahead of time. This way, you will always know where they are if you need them at a later date. There are also apps you can use to digitally capture your paper receipts!

20. **Create a purchasing plan and stick to it.**

Come up with a specific goal before each shopping trip, such as what type of things you need or want to buy. Then write down only what you need to buy for that specific shopping trip. Make sure to include a reasonable spending limit for each different item. Take your list to the store with you, with only the amount of money needed for each item on your list. You can look at other things, but you are not allowed to buy anything that isn't on your list, no matter how enticing or cheap it may be. You should consult your plan and objective repeatedly while shopping to make sure you don't veer off track.

21. **Pay yourself an allowance.**

By paying yourself an allowance, you are essentially setting up barriers that make it harder for you to spend money. In order to do this properly, start by looking at your budget for each different category of expenses so you can see how much you can afford to spend on these items each month. After you come up with an exact amount, go to your bank and take out the exact amount of cash. Then put the money in separate envelopes marked with all of your different categories. Always keep these in a secure and hidden location. When you need to buy something, you can take cash out of the envelope specified for the specific category. When the envelope is empty, you can't buy anything else for that category until the next month starts. Consider these envelopes your *allowance* for the month. This allowance helps you stay within your budget because it shows you what you can, and cannot, afford to spend each month. This strategy helps remind you of appropriate limits while curbing your impulsive spending habits.

22. **Learn to budget.**

You must devise an ADHD money management plan by learning how to budget. A budget will make a significant impact on your life in a positive way, no matter how challenging it is to create in the beginning. A budget allows you to know exactly how much money you can spend each month. It also allows you to pre-plan how you want to spend your money, down to the last penny. This allows you to only purchase the things that are the most important to you rather than spending impulsively. You are also able to track your spending by seeing which categories each expense goes to. Instead of viewing a budget as a punishment or a chore, understand that it empowers you while providing structure.

23. **Reward yourself in another way.**

What *else* makes you feel good? Make a list of "feel good" activities that you can substitute for spending money. Try things like
- Taking a hot bath
- Reading a book
- Listening to an audiobook
- Listening to music
- Calling that friend you've been meaning to call for a while now.
- Spending some quality time with your pets
- Helping someone else with your gifts (such as helping kids with their homework)

Substituting one thing for another may seem elementary, but you'll be pleasantly surprised that giving yourself joy in other ways is an effective method for filling the void left behind when you resist the urge to spend money you don't have – on things you don't need!

Chapter 5: 5 Hacks to Control Impulsive ADHD

The first step in controlling your impulsivity is to seek the help and support of a mental health professional. They will be able to help you create and maintain a treatment plan for ADHD. There is also a lot you can do on your own to improve your impulsivity control and quality of life when you are an active participant in your treatment regimen.

Your individual ADHD symptoms vary based on your circumstances and personality type. Impulsivity is basically your emotions driving your behavior, which looks like an unpredicted course of action that is not based on any logic whatsoever.

These impulsive actions can even go against your own habits or plans and can become harmful to yourself or those around you. Some examples of harmful impulsive behaviors include:

- Hopping from one activity to the next, or trying to handle three simultaneously
- Going out to have one drink, and coming home with someone you don't know
- Saying things you later regret, or constantly interrupting conversations

- Getting impatient while driving, and cursing in front of everyone
- Going shopping for one item, then returning home with endless bags

Do any of these examples sound familiar to you? Have any of them happened to you personally? In order to properly control your impulses, you must first understand the functioning behind your ADHD so you can put practices into place. What are the common negative consequences? Where and when are you the most impulsive? How does your impulsivity manifest?

Because no two adults with impulsive ADHD are identical, you must understand your particular "flavor" of ADHD and how it affects your life. Begin by taking notes in order to identify the particulars of your impulse control challenges so you can become more aware.

You will eventually find a system that works best for you. You can begin keeping inventory of all the hacks that work best for you. Let's look at some examples of how you can begin:

- Identity negative consequences of recent impulsive behaviors
- Identify positive consequences of recent impulsive behaviors
- List recent behaviors that other people consider impulsive in you

- List recent behaviors that you consider to be impulsive
- Select some impulsive behaviors that might be the most harmful to you or others
- Pinpoint the places where you most frequently become impulsive

After you are able to understand the functioning of your ADHD, then you can better understand the five impulse control techniques listed in the hacks below.

1. **Stop the action.**

    Oftentimes, it is hard to resist your impulses because you don't give yourself the time to stop and think in order to measure your actions and words. You must use both foresight and hindsight in order to assess a situation so you can determine what you should do or say. There are different ways you can go about doing this:
    - **Choose a slow-talking model:** Always *slow it down* when you are having a conversation. Practice speaking slowly in front of a mirror. Rather than being swept away by your impulses, your frontal lobes will have a chance to gain some traction and become engaged.
    - **Make a list of the situations in which you are most likely to behave impulsively:** When you are about to

enter one of the identified situations, give yourself a few thoughtful seconds by performing any of the following actions:
    - Put your finger over your mouth for a few seconds, as if you are considering what you're going to say.
    - Imagine locking your mouth with a key to prevent yourself from speaking.
    - Before you answer someone, slowly inhale, slowly exhale, put on a thoughtful expression, then say to yourself "Well, let me think about that."
    - Paraphrase what your family member or boss said to you: "You're asking me to…" or "Oh, so you want to know about…"
2. **See the past… and then move forward.**

    Do you beat yourself up repeatedly for making the same mistakes? Are you often confused about what to do or what is going to happen when a problem arises? Due to ADHD, you have a weak nonverbal working memory, meaning you don't typically draw on hindsight to guide your actions. You are also not likely good at recognizing the subtle aspects of a problem or the various tools you might use to solve it. You may also find it hard to defer gratification because you can't call up the mental image of the prize in the future. You must learn to do all of these things in order to stick to healthy eating or quit spending impulsively. You need a specific tool to ensure that what you learned from the past is always easily accessible when you need it again in the future. One example of this includes:

- **Picture what happened the last time you were in a sticky situation:** You should be able to *stop the action* after adhering to strategy number one, listed above. After that step, picture an actual visual device, such as a computer monitor, minicam, or flat-screen TV. Visualize on that imaginary screen what happened the last time you were in a similar situation. Try to let the past unfold in colorful detail, as if you are filming or replaying the scenario. The more you practice this, the more automatic and habitual it will become. You will find that more of these "videos" will pop into your brain from your memory bank. For example, you may think "I felt guilty when I bought myself those expensive shoes last month because then I couldn't afford to buy my daughter new school shoes." or "Wow, everyone laughed at me the last time I interrupted the meeting with a joke, instead of laughing at the punch line."

3. **Feel the future.**

Many adults with ADHD experience time blindness, which causes you to forget the purpose of your tasks or be uninspired to finish anything. You may need some convincing to keep moving toward your goal, especially if there is no one there to dangle something sparkly and shiny in front of you. This is why the second strategy is so important, as it helps you become adept at handling similar situations in the future as you learn from your moments in the past. However, that will not always be enough. Some things must get done simply because they are the right thing to do. ADHD makes it difficult for people to grasp the moral imperative for completing a task or project. Imagining the negative consequence of *not* doing something is often not a strong enough motivator for people with ADHD. Instead, you will likely have more success when you imagine how great it will feel to finish your task or reach your goal. An example of this strategy put into action looks like:

- **Asking yourself how you will feel after you complete your project:** Work hard to feel whatever the emotion is right then and there as you contemplate your goal. You may answer with self-satisfaction, pride, or even happiness from anticipating finishing the task. Every time you sit down to work on the project, continue trying to imagine the future outcome. You can even cut out pictures of the rewards you hope to earn after the project is completed and place them around for you to see while working. These photos will make the emotions of your anticipation become even more vivid as they enhance the potency of your own imagination.

4. **Break it down...and make it matter.**

The future likely seems so far away, so a project that requires a significant amount of time can often prove so elusive that you feel overwhelmed. This is especially true when it has to be done in a sequence of steps or includes waiting periods.

You will likely look for an escape route by passing on the responsibility to a co-worker or calling in sick to avoid the project. Try to avoid projects that are most likely going to cause you to shut down. Do complex projects overwhelm you? Do you have trouble working without direct supervision? Do you panic when someone gives you a deadline that is months away? You may need some external motivation if you answered yes to any of these questions, including:

- **Break down long-term goals or tasks into smaller steps:** If an end-of-the-day

deadline seems remote to you, try the following steps:
- Break your task into half-hour or one-hour chunks of work. To keep your attention focused, write down what you need to accomplish during each period, and run a highlighter over each step as you work on it.
- Social judgment allows you to get more things done because most people care what others think about them. So make yourself accountable to another person in order to double your chances of success. Work with a spouse, partner, or co-worker.
- Do the following four things after finishing each smaller task: 1) take a short break; 2) congratulate yourself; 3) give yourself a reward or privilege you enjoy; 4) e-mail or call a friend to tell them what you just accomplished.

5. **Keep a sense of humor.**

Even though ADHD is a serious mental health condition, you don't always have to be so serious.
- **Learn to put a smile on your face:** Then say, "Well, there goes my ADHD

acting up or talking again. My mistake. Sorry about that. I have to try to do something about that in the future." You have done four very important things when you say this:
- You owned the mistake.
- You explained why the mistake happened.
- You made no excuse by blaming others, but rather, you apologized.
- You promised to try to do better next time.

If you do these things, you will keep your friends, as well as your self-esteem. Blaming others, disowning your ADHD conduct, or not trying to do better next time will cost you. When you make ADHD an all-encompassing disability, your family and friends will treat it that way as well. If you approach it with a sense of humor instead, you will notice that everyone else will too. It's all about how you approach and treat your ADHD. Everyone else will follow your lead.

Conclusion

One of the most common symptoms of ADHD is impulsivity. This is especially true for those with the hyperactive-impulsive presentation. There are several areas where adults with ADHD are commonly impulsive, including their financial responsibility, decision-making, and emotions.

Impulsive ADHD is defined as a pattern of behavior that is characterized by serious and chronic problems with impulsivity. People with impulsive ADHD have trouble waiting their turn, may act without thinking, and often interrupt others. They also have difficulty controlling their emotions and sustaining attention.

Some common examples of impulsive behaviors for adults with ADHD include the following:

- Lack of self-control at checkout counters, including buying more than you intended
- Struggling to stay on an important task after being suddenly struck with a great idea
- Making big, sometimes even life-changing, decisions without thinking them through
- Blurting out inappropriate, ill-timed, or even hurtful things in conversation

Additional impulsive choices might include things such as risky sexual behaviors, overspending, substance abuse, or overindulging with food and drinks.

Even though we do not know the exact cause of impulsive ADHD, we have been able to identify some risk factors, such as:

- Maternal smoking, drug use, or alcohol use during pregnancy
- Brain injury
- Low birth weight
- Exposure to toxins, such as lead

There is no single "quick fix" that will magically turn you into a careful, calculated decision-maker overnight. However, with the proper support and practice, you can build new skills that will help you improve.

There are several treatment options available if you have impulsive ADHD, including mindfulness practices, medication, psychotherapy, and support groups. You can also be an active participant in your treatment plan by following the hacks listed in the above chapters.

To recap chapter 1, we looked at 37 daily hacks to maximize your strengths. Some of the hacks included in this chapter were:

- Calm down when you begin to feel stressed or emotional

- Keep your things organized
- Harness the power of hyperfocus
- Keep your to-do list printed out in front of you
- Check your calendar twice a day

Then, in chapter 2, we discussed 13 hacks to manage impulsivity. Some of the hacks in this chapter included:

- Track your history
- Create obstacles
- Plan ahead
- Identify weak spots
- Learn emotional management skills

Next, in chapter 3, we learned 19 self-help hacks to improve impulsivity. Some of the hacks included in this chapter were:

- Indulge when down
- Practice gratitude
- Take off your cape
- Increase dopamine naturally
- Inhale essential oils

In chapter 4, we went over 23 hacks to improve impulsive spending. Some of the hacks included in this chapter were:

- Learn to budget
- Pay yourself an allowance

- Create a purchasing plan and stick to it
- Keep your receipts
- Substitute other behaviors

Finally, in chapter 5, we looked at 5 hacks to control impulsive ADHD. Some of the hacks included in this chapter were:

- Break it down… and make it matter
- Keep a sense of humor
- See the past, then move forward
- Stop the action
- Feel the future

You now have 97 impulsivity hacks at your disposal to add to your current ADHD treatment plan. All of these hacks are meant to be used alongside your treatment plan, and not to be used in place of.

Instead of trying to remember all 97 hacks at once, I would encourage you to start with a few hacks. Try those and see how they work out with you. Then you can always come back to the book to re-learn some new hacks as needed.

Take it one day at a time. You will not simply get over your impulsive behaviors over night. It will take time and patience. But you now have the tools needed in order to do the work.

**Stop Procrastinating
47 Hacks to Get Your Ass in Gear**

Kristen Thrasher

Table of Contents

Introduction
Chapter 1: Procrastination at its Heart
Chapter 2: The Link Between Procrastination and ADHD
Chapter 3: Three Minute Procrastination Challenge
Chapter 4: 15 Hacks to Improve Procrastination at Work
Chapter 5: 14 Hacks to Overcome Procrastination at Home
Chapter 6: 18 Hacks to Overcome Procrastination in Your Personal Life
Conclusion

74

Introduction

What type of procrastinator are *you*? According to Ali Schiller and Marissa Boisvert, co-owners of Accountability Works, a mindfulness-based coaching company, there are four specific types of procrastinators.

1. The Performer
2. The Self-Deprecator
3. The Overbooker
4. The Novelty Seeker

Let's look a little closer at each type and maybe you can see which resonates most with you. Who knows? Maybe you're a combination of more than one!

1. The performer who says, "I work well when there's a deadline"
This procrastinator created the ability to focus by forcing the time to complete a task to nearly run out. Often, an underlying cause for this can be perfectionism. When there is a time crunch, you can't afford to perform a task to your ridiculously high standards, right? Therefore, it gets done however you manage

to do it, but not perfectly, and that's forgiven. Regardless of the root cause, habitually stressing yourself out with last-minute deadlines is not pleasant or productive.

Your biggest issue: Starting a project.

Your solution: Flip the script and set a start date. Focusing on the beginning of a project rather than the deadline removes pressure and allows you to start, which is your problem.

2. The self-deprecator who says, "I'm feeling so lazy and blah now"

In reality and despite what they are saying, this procrastinator is not lazy. They work so hard that when they *don't* do something, they are especially hard on themselves. These procrastinators blame their lack of progress on laziness or stubbornness instead of just admitting that they need a break. What they really need is more self-care and perhaps a look at how much they are taking on.

Your biggest issue: Giving yourself a break. You are probably already shaking your head and saying, "I don't have time to rest!"

Your solution: Recharge. Take a long lunch, get a massage, or walk outside on your break to get some fresh air and recharge your batteries. Even small changes in your environment can help you return to work with a fresh mindset.

3. The overbooker who says, "I'm so busy"
This procrastinator is an expert at filling their time and is often overwhelmed. "I'm so busy" is a common excuse. However, busy people tend to get things done. So where does that leave us? When busy-ness comes up as an excuse for not doing something, it's often an indication of avoidance. Rather than facing something head on or saying you would rather not do something, it's easier to put the blame on doing other important work.

Your biggest issue: Creating chaos to avoid facing what you ought to be doing instead (usually not other tasks).

Your solution: Take a moment to look inside yourself. Ask yourself: What am I really avoiding? Why is my life chaotic?

4. The novelty seeker who says, "I just had the best idea!"
This procrastinator has a terminal case of Shiny Object Syndrome. They're always coming up with new projects to take on — and then tiring of them quickly and moving on. This

procrastinator lacks follow-through. They are great at making decisions and taking action. However, they end up inadvertently losing a lot of time and burning out because not working in one direction long enough yields no results.

Your biggest issue: Completion.

Your solution: Capture all of your ideas on a spreadsheet, but promise yourself you will not even start them until you finish what you're currently working on.

Chapter 1: Procrastination at its Heart

Procrastination is defined as putting off tasks, either until the last minute or past their deadline. Some researchers go even further to say that procrastination is a form of self-regulation failure, which is characterized by the irrational delay of tasks despite many potentially negative consequences. There are multiple causes for the complex behavior, including:

1. Disinterest
2. External stress
3. Perfectionism
4. Feeling overwhelmed
5. Need for time-management techniques
6. Inexperience

In the United States, around 20 percent of all adults suffer from chronic procrastination. Regardless of how well-organized you are, chances are that you have found yourself wasting away hours shopping online, watching TV, or updating your Facebook status rather than spending that time on school or work-related projects.

Because procrastination causes negative self-perception and impedes productivity, it is known to cause more distress in the long run. Procrastination is a learned behavior that can be overcome with practice. The key to maximizing your work performance and boosting your overall mental and physical health is to focus your attention. This can lead to happiness and increased job satisfaction.

Not everyone who puts off a task is a procrastinator. Many people will briefly delay an important task for a good reason. Some legitimate reasons for putting off a task can include when you have a more important assignment come up or if a loved one is sick.

Chronic procrastination is much different. You may have an underlying issue with procrastination if you:

1. Fill your day with low-priority tasks rather than completing big-priority assignments
2. Leave an important item on your to-do list until the last possible minute
3. Unnecessarily check your email several times while working on an assignment
4. Wait until you are in the "right mood" or until the "right time" to work on a task
5. Start a high-priority task and then break for coffee or another similar distraction

Procrastination can have a major impact on your grades, your job, and your personal life. It can cause you to avoid homework assignments, put off finishing a project for work, or even ignore everyday household chores. However, rather than a sign of a serious problem, procrastination is often a tendency that people give in to on occasion.

There are several factors that can contribute to procrastination. Of the biggest factors is the notion that you have to feel motivated or inspired to work on a task at that moment.

Many people assume that projects won't take nearly as long to finish as they really do. You can create a false sense of security when you tell yourself you still have plenty of time to complete your tasks.

In all reality, when you wait until you are in the right frame of mind to begin certain tasks, especially the undesirable ones, you will likely find that the right time never comes along. This causes you to never accomplish or complete your tasks.

Some other contributing factors that can cause procrastination can include the following:

- **Academics:** Research has shown that procrastination is especially prevalent among students. A 2007 meta analysis published in the *Psychological Bulletin* found that 80 to 95 percent of college students displayed procrastination on a regular basis, especially when it comes to completing coursework or other assignments. Research also shows that there are some major cognitive distortions that lead to academic procrastination. For instance, many students will overestimate how motivated they will be in the future and how much time they will have left to perform tasks, while underestimating how long a certain task will take to complete. Many students also mistakenly assume they need to be in the right frame of mind to work on a task.
- **Present Bias:** This phenomenon means that people tend to be more motivated by immediate gratification than by long-term rewards. This is exactly why procrastination

feels so good at the moment. For example, the immediate reward of staying on the couch and watching TV is much more appealing than the long-term reward of finishing your paper, which would take much longer to complete.

- **Depression:** Feelings of helplessness and a lack of energy will make it difficult to start, and actually finish, even the simplest tasks. Depression is also known to lead to self-doubt. You are more likely to put off a project when you feel insecure about your abilities or are unable to figure out how to begin the project.
- **Obsessive-Compulsive Disorder (OCD):** People with OCD normally have a propensity toward indecision, which causes them to procrastinate instead of making an affirmative decision. OCD is also linked with maladaptive perfectionism, which causes people to doubt if they are doing something correctly, worry about others' expectations, and have fears about making new mistakes.
- **Attention-Deficit/Hyperactivity Disorder (ADHD):** It can be hard to get started on a task when you are distracted by internal thoughts or outside stimuli, especially if that task is either not interesting or difficult for you.

While procrastination in itself is not a mental illness, it may be symptomatic of an underlying mental health condition, such as ADHD, depression, or OCD.

People come up with a plethora of different rationalizations or excuses to justify their procrastination tendencies. Research has shown 15 key reasons why people say they procrastinate, including:

1. Not caring if something gets done or not
2. Not caring when something gets done
3. Being in the habit of waiting until the last minute
4. Not wanting to do something
5. Not feeling in the mood to do it
6. Not knowing what needs to be done
7. Not knowing how to do something
8. Forgetting
9. Believing that you work better under pressure
10. Blaming poor health or sickness
11. Thinking that you can finish it at the last minute
12. Lacking the initiative to get started
13. Delaying one task in favor of working on another
14. Needing time to think about the task
15. Waiting for the right moment

There are two types of procrastination, including active and passive procrastinators. The differences include:

- **Active procrastinators:** Delay the task purposefully because working under pressure allows them to feel motivated and challenged.

- **Passive procrastinators:** Delay the task because they have trouble making decisions and acting on them.

Other researchers define the even more types of self-delay based on different behavioral styles of procrastination, including:

- **Defier:** Doesn't believe someone should dictate their time schedule
- **Dreamer:** Puts off tasks because they are not good at paying attention to detail
- **Perfectionist:** Puts off tasks out of the fear of not being able to complete the task perfectly
- **Overdoer:** Takes on too much and struggles with finding time to start and complete task
- **Worrier:** Puts off tasks out of fear of change or leaving the comfort of what is known
- **Crisis-maker:** Puts off tasks because they like working under pressure

Non-procrastinators are able to focus on the task that needs to be done. They can have a stronger personal identity and are less concerned about social esteem (how others like them) as opposed to self-esteem (how we feel about ourselves).

People who don't procrastinate tend to have the personality trait known as conscientiousness, which is one of the broad dispositions identified by the Big Five theory of personality. People who are high in conscientiousness also tend to be high in other areas, such as persistence, self-discipline, and personal responsibility.

Procrastination only becomes a more serious issue in cases where it becomes chronic and begins to have a serious impact on a person's daily life. In these instances, it is a major part of their lifestyle, and not just a matter of having poor time management skills. Some examples of this include people who don't start working on big projects until the night before the deadline, file their income tax return late, pay their bills late, or delay gift shopping until the day before a birthday.

Unfortunately, this procrastination can have a serious impact on several different life areas, including a person's mental health and professional, financial, and social well-being. A person can offer suffer from:

- Increased burden placed on social relationships
- Higher levels of stress and illness
- Consequences of delinquent bills and income tax returns
- Resentment from family, friends, fellow students, and co-workers

While everyone procrastinates from time to time, ADHD procrastination is a totally different thing. It is much more extreme, more regular, more damaging, harder to control, and paired with other symptoms. For people with ADHD, procrastination frequently occurs repeatedly and causes problems at work, home, or in your personal life. Even if you recognize that procrastination *is* what is causing these problems, you likely feel as if it is out of your control to break the pattern.

In many cases, ADHD symptoms could happen to anyone. When multiple types of these behaviors occur repeatedly and cause serious problems, you may be suffering from ADHD. Therefore, procrastination itself does not necessarily suggest ADHD. Rather, it does raise questions when it is combined with other ADHD-related behaviors.

In this book, we are going to start by taking a deeper look at the link between ADHD and procrastination. Then, we give you a three minute procrastination challenge to complete. After this, we get into the procrastination hacks divided up into hacks to overcome procrastination at work, at home, and in your personal life.

Are you ready to finally be able to solve the reason behind your procrastination tendencies in different areas of your life? Have you been looking for some hacks to be able to put into practice, but you just haven't known where to start?

My advice for you is to read everything with an open mind. The hacks listed in the chapters ahead will never work if you do not give them your all. Make sure not to procrastinate after you finish this book. You must put the hacks in this book to use right away. Let's dig in!

Chapter 2: The Link Between Procrastination and ADHD

There is a complex relationship between procrastination and ADHD. While there is no direct link between the two, some of the ADHD symptoms can lead to procrastination. Everyone has a natural tendency to procrastinate occasionally. Many of us will put off tasks we don't want to do until tomorrow. Sometimes we set aside tasks because we are waiting until we have more energy to tackle them on a new day. Other times we simply set aside tasks until we are less overwhelmed with all of our other responsibilities.

The problem in those with ADHD is that they may procrastinate in an extreme manner that occurs repeatedly, known as chronic procrastination. This then leads to severe problems at work, home, and even in your personal life. Even though many people with ADHD can admit that their procrastination is significant and causing repeated issues, they will find it challenging to break the pattern.

ADHD is a neurodevelopmental disorder that is known by symptoms such as hyperactivity, impulsivity, and inattention. According to the Centers for Disease Control and Preventions (CDC) approximately 9 percent of all children have been diagnosed with ADHD.

ADHD is generally diagnosed during childhood. However, it affects adults as well. In fact, the National Institute of Mental Health (NIMH) claims that approximately 4.4 percent of adults suffer from ADHD. However, this number is likely much larger, as it is common for adult ADHD to go undiagnosed and untreated.

While healthcare professionals do not currently acknowledge procrastination as an ADHD symptom, they do believe that ADHD symptoms may lead to procrastination. Some of these symptoms include:

- Having difficulty organizing tasks
- Becoming easily distracted
- Being forgetful
- Making careless mistakes with either school or work
- Avoiding tasks that require large amounts of mental effort

We know that people procrastinate for several different reasons, including their desire to engage in activities that are more interesting. For people with ADHD, procrastination is strongly influenced by the symptoms of their condition.

Even though it is very common, procrastination is not actually recognized as an official diagnostic symptom of ADHD. In a 2014 study, researchers found that procrastination was only connected to inattention, and not impulsivity as well.

Some research also suggests that procrastination will serve as a compensation strategy for adults and teens who have ADHD. This means that when someone is faced with a challenging task, procrastination will offer them a way to stop dealing with whatever unpleasant problem they feel is too difficult for their abilities.

While the factors that contribute to procrastination are varied and complex, problems with executive functioning play a key role. Executive functioning skills are the mental skills that are needed to organize, plan, initiate, and then complete tasks. These skills include things such as time management, self control, and working memory.

Because those with ADHD have difficulty maintaining a consistent focus for long periods of time, they may be led to delay the completion of tasks. They may also believe that the job requires more mental effort than they can afford or they may simply become quickly distracted.

Imbalances in motivation can occur in people with ADHD as they tend to hyperfocus on tasks they find interesting, but will procrastinate over tasks that seem tedious. They may also experience a resistance to taking action due to some emotional conflict related to the task at hand.

Another aspect of ADHD that can lead to procrastination is time management. This can include remembering all of the elements involved in completing a task and having difficulty establishing priorities.

Some people with ADHD will also find mental tasks daunting, especially for tasks that require a lot of effort over a long period of time. This can cause people to put off tasks, or simply avoid them altogether.

Many adults with ADHD struggle with chronic procrastination, which can cause problems at work when their job responsibilities are not completed until the last possible second. It can cause problems in relationships when you continue to put off others, which makes them feel unimportant. And it can also cause financial stress at home when bills are paid late or when balancing the checkbook is constantly delayed.

Procrastination can also lead to negative emotions and moods as well as low self-esteem. This failure to complete tasks can lead to feelings of shame, guilt, and frustration, which can also contribute to the tendency of putting off tasks in the first place.

Research also suggests that people with more serious ADHD symptoms experience more procrastination, as well as internalizing symptoms, such as anxiety and depression. Helping people address their procrastination tendencies can help resolve some of the negative internalizing emotions that can occur in ADHD, such as depression, sadness, shame, anxiety and guilt.

There are a variety of ADHD-related factors that lead to chronic procrastination, including forgetfulness, distractibility, disorganization, and problems with time management, sequencing, and prioritizing. A person may also naturally avoid those tasks in which they experience repeated frustrations in order to avoid the negative feelings that can come up while working on those tasks.

Some of the factors that can often be at play in the relationship between procrastination and ADHD include:

- **Problems getting started:** Simply getting started on a task can be very difficult for an adult with ADHD, especially if that task is not intrinsically interesting. It can be hard to even begin the task when you are so distracted by either internal thoughts or outside stimuli. Sometimes the biggest challenge is just figuring out how or where to start. Problems with organization come into play as you struggle to plan, prioritize, and sequence tasks that need to be done in order to begin and stay on track with the task at hand.
- **Getting sidetracked:** You may find that you quickly become sidetracked by something more interesting, so the original task becomes even further delayed. It is extremely difficult to regulate your attention when you suffer from ADHD. You may find that it is hard to sustain your attention, when you are able to become

focused on a task, because your mind wanders. When you aren't very interested or stimulated by the task at hand, it can be hard to stay motivated, alert, and on track. You may likely delay getting to tasks until the very last minute, especially when they are boring or tedious, at which point you either feel such pressure that you are able to motivate yourself to finally complete the task, or you become stuck not completing the task at all and are forced to face the consequences.

- **Last-minute propulsion:** Putting off things until the very last minute can create an emergency-type situation, or an urgency of sorts, for some people with ADHD that helps propel them forward to successfully get the job done. You may be better able to focus and complete the task when there is a fast-approaching deadline, or the immediacy of the negative consequences that will occur if the deadline is not met. The biggest problem with this is that the urgency can create stress and anxiety, which takes a tremendous toll on you and everyone around you. What's more, these last-minute rush jobs also tend not to be as high quality as they could have potentially been without the procrastination.
- **Sense of paralysis and feeling overwhelmed:** You may experience a painful sense of paralysis when faced with a task. You may want to get started but become unable to

make any forward progress on the task. You may experience a crushing sense of pressure. You likely just can't get started, even with as much as you know the job needs to get done.
- **Impaired sense of time:** You might put off a task if you have trouble estimating the time it will take to complete because you will believe you are still allowing enough time to finish the task. ADHD can also make it difficult to track the passage of time, so deadlines may sneak up on you before you even realize it. Consider my book on *Time Blindness* if you believe this is one of your areas for improvement.
- **Fear of failure:** There can be so much anxiety associated with starting the task that these feelings will create an even greater obstacle. For instance, the fear of imperfection, fear or failure, and fear of not doing the task right can all add to procrastination.

Perfectionism is defined as someone who demands an extraordinarily high, or even faultless, level of performance of themselves. Perfectionism procrastination can occur when a person puts off doing something simply because they fear that they will not be able to maintain their self-imposed level of perfectionism that they so desire. Rather than facing these premature feelings of failure, they will likely decide to put off the project altogether.

There are three types of procrastination based on the area of life to which it applies, including everyday procrastination, academic procrastination, and decisional procrastination. Perfectionism procrastination most typically occurs with academic procrastination.

Academic procrastination sometimes results from a person who believes they are unable to navigate the significant mental challenges they may need to face. When it comes to perfectionism, the person may also worry that they will not be able to finish the project as well as they should.

One example includes students who procrastinate about studying for an exam. They may put off the task because they do not want to face the possibility that they will not be able to learn all of the material.

The academic task that most often causes people to procrastinate is writing. Many people with ADHD believe writing to be a mentally strenuous task that will take them longer to complete than they are able to comfortably manage. Insecurity about one's writing skills may contribute to the lack of desire to begin the writing assignment.

Procrastination is frequently viewed as harmful because it can affect several different aspects of a person's well-being. Therefore, procrastination could have an even more significant impact on those suffering from ADHD, as their academic performance also contributes to these factors.

People with ADHD are more likely to have reduced levels of well-being and lower self-esteem, particularly because they are more likely to struggle in school due to procrastination. Coincidentally, low self-esteem is very common in people suffering from ADHD,even though there are other factors that can impact this aside from the potential tendency for procrastination.

Medical professionals are able to help people manage their ADHD with a combination of both occupational therapy and medication. Occupational therapy is an excellent form of treatment for those who procrastinate frequently.

An occupational therapist is a trained professional that can offer various solutions to the underlying issues that cause people with ADHD to procrastinate. With the proper amount of help, a person with ADHD is able to tackle their to-do lists by using the new strategies and skills that work with their ADHD instead of against it.

An occupational therapist will work with someone to help them develop the required discipline needed to finish tasks through to completion, as well as helping them address practical time management skills.

Many people with ADHD find that quickly after beginning a new project, they are fully immersed and lose all track of time, known as hyperfocus. This is not necessarily a negative thing, especially when the person is working on something productive. However, hyperfocus becomes problematic when a person becomes engrossed in a leisurely activity that is completely unrelated to the required project.

An occupational therapist can also help those with ADHD discover their reasons behind avoiding activities. After they fully understand why they are putting off projects, they will be able to work with their occupational therapist to improve the skills they need to further explore their reasoning.

Another way that people are able to manage their ADHD symptoms is through medication. There are two types of medication approved for ADHD treatment which are stimulants and nonstimulants. For those who experience procrastination, stimulants appear to be more beneficial, as they may help people with their time management issues.

Ultimately, there is no direct correlation between procrastination and ADHD. However, we do know that some of the ADHD symptoms can lead an individual to procrastinate. Even though procrastination is not a symptom that is specific to ADHD, people with ADHD do often experience it due to the other ADHD symptoms.

Chapter 3: Three Minute Procrastination Challenge

Procrastination can affect many different areas of your life. It can also be a daily struggle for many people. For example, maybe you procrastinate on exercising, so you tell yourself you will put off starting until tomorrow. Or maybe you struggle with getting started on a project, so you decide to put that off for later too.

Even worse, maybe you procrastinate on taking action on the big dream you have had for years, so you keep putting it off as well.

If this sounds familiar to you, I'd like for you to try the procrastination challenge today. Right now. There are six small steps, but you must do all six of them, without procrastinating.

Three Minute Procrastination Challenge
1. Read the five quick procrastination hacks listed below. It will only take about 3 minutes total. Don't put it off until later. Read them right now.
2. Think of something simple that you have been putting off. Only think of one small task.
3. Pick one of the hacks listed below – the one that stands out to you the most. It doesn't matter which one.

4. Try it.
5. Accomplish your simple task. Excellent work!
6. Do it again tomorrow.

Procrastination hacks to choose from:
1. **The "(10+2)*5" Hack**

    This hack is an excellent place to start. It is a shortened version of the Pomodoro Technique. There are four small steps included in this hack.
    - Pick your task
    - Set your timer for 10 minutes. You can only work on the task at hand
    - Give yourself a 2 minute break.
    - Repeat the second and third step 5 times.

2. **The "Airplane" Hack**

    This hack is for everyone who spends a lot of time responding to phone calls, text messages, social-media updates, and emails. There are only three steps to this hack.
    - Pretend you are on an airplane (one without Wi-Fi).
    - Put your phone in airplane mode. Pause your email.
    - Accomplish your task

3. **The "Super-Tiny Tasks" Hack**

    This hack is great for any intimidating or big tasks. All you have to do is take the big action or task and break it down into super-tiny, easy tasks. For example, let's assume your

BIG task is working out at the gym. The *super-tiny* tasks involved would be:
- Put on your tennis shoes.
- Get into your car.
- Drive to the gym.
- Stretch.
- Workout for 15 minutes.

4. The "Scheduled Stress Time" Hack

If you are someone who is constantly anxious or stressed out, you will enjoy this hack, even if it sounds slightly weird at first. You will typically be less effective when you are stressed, which leads to you being less productive as well. By using this hack, you are accepting that while stress is a part of your life, it doesn't have to be all of your life.

- Schedule a short block of time, around 20 minutes.
- Give yourself permission to give into all of your stress.

It can be extremely helpful to write down all of the crazy thoughts and ideas that come up as a way to purge them before getting back to your tasks.

5. The "30-10" Hack.

Basically, with this hack you will set a timer for 30 minutes and work as much as you can until the timer goes off. Then, set another timer for 10 minutes. However, this time do something that you really want to do, such as watching TV or checking your social news

feed. Repeat this process as often as necessary. The most important thing to remember is to stick to your timer - don't go beyond your 10 minute break, and don't stop working on the task until the 30 minutes are up. For example:
- Set a timer for 30 minutes.
- Work on your task until the timer goes off.
- Set another time for 10 minutes.
- Do something you really want to do until the timer goes off.
- Repeat all steps until you have finished your task.

Now, it is your turn to take the procrastination challenge! Ready? Go get it done! Then, you can read the rest of the procrastination hacks in this book. This procrastination challenge will work with any of the other hacks. Simply pick a hack, find a task you need to accomplish, and get started.

You can use the same procrastination hack over and over. Or, you can try different hacks until you find your favorites. You can use the hacks listed in this book alone or you can combine multiple ones. Make sure to personalize each hack for whatever works best for you personally.

Chapter 4: 15 Hacks to Improve Procrastination at Work

Many of us struggle with procrastination, be it waiting until the last minute to turn in a class assignment or putting off a work project. Procrastination causes you to plan to do something that you want to do, but you may not feel like it or even have the energy to begin the project. When you procrastinate, you understand that it is a bad idea to put off the project, but you find yourself doing it anyway. People can be more prone to procrastination when they are creative or struggle with focus.

Procrastination can lead to increased stress, which means that you are not always thinking clearly when it is time to work on your task or project. However, sometimes you may feel it is just easier to work under extreme pressure, even with all of the known consequences. While many people may genuinely believe that they do their best work when they are close to their deadline, they can also be more likely to experience increased stress or emotional distress due to the habitual practice of waiting until the last minute.

In this chapter, we are going to examine 15 hacks to overcome procrastination at work. You will have serious consequences if you don't learn how to overcome procrastination in your workplace. You could even potentially lose your job if you don't step up. As you go through this chapter, think about which hacks you want to try first and which hacks would work best for you.

1. **Schedule non-negotiable windows of time.**
Schedule more challenging tasks or projects to help you complete them earlier. It is important to set yourself concrete goals on when you should be finished. Create mini-deadlines for yourself that you must reach no matter what, rather than focusing on the actual deadline of your task. For example, if you need to create a slideshow presentation for next week, set yourself a goal to finish two slides per day before the actual deadline arises. You can use a mobile app or planner to schedule specific tasks in order to give you a better sense of all the tasks you have coming up and when you need to have certain aspects of each task completed. View your schedule in terms of non-negotiable windows of time. Always finish every assignment in your planner by the deadline you gave yourself, instead of the actual deadline.
2. **Eliminate distractions.**
It is crucial that you avoid temptation in order to finish all of your tasks. For example, you are more likely to procrastinate later in the day when you have frequently checked your

social media and phone messenger or stopped to chat with your co-worker. To ensure that you remain focused solely on the current task at hand, silence your phone, blocking social media websites or apps, and imposing other specific restrictions on yourself. First example, wait until your lunch break instead of telling your exciting news to a coworker first thing in the morning. This way you can have something to look forward to and give yourself a break when the agreed upon time arises.Clear off your desk, turn all distractions off your laptop, clear away all web pages, and silent all email notifications. Do anything you can think of to rid yourself of distractions in order to make it easier on yourself

3. **Set a deadline.**

    One of the best tools for getting projects done is setting a deadline. You are more likely to complete the task when you set a deadline. This hack has plenty of uses, even if the pressure of a deadline isn't felt until after the deadline, as is the case with some people.

4. **The "Schedule It Last Minute" Hack**

    This hack from Leo Babauta will make your procrastination an asset, at least in small doses. This is for those of you who have an absolute deadline for a task that will take right at an hour to complete. Schedule this task so you don't actually begin until about an hour before that deadline. It is wise to give yourself a 30-minute cushion just to be safe. The point behind this is that when you have absolutely no padded time in your schedule, you have no choice but to get your tasks done without procrastinating. An example of this is how productive you are the day before you go on vacation.

5. **Love your work.**

    Sometimes we procrastinate simply because we don't like what we need to do. Maybe consider a different line of work, or at least a different job, if that is the case for you. Either way, seek to do things that you love, even while at your current job. If you do not think you will enjoy that task for the time being, find a different job task that is more fun for you (as long as you stick to the tasks, and not decide to play video games or watch TV).

6. **Do your most important task first.**

    Create a rule for yourself that you must always do your most important task first, even before you read your feeds or check your email. If you do your most important task first thing in the morning, no matter what happens after that, you will already have a very productive day. This is especially important if you have been procrastinating on an important task for some time. Simply don't allow yourself to do anything else until that most important thing is done.

7. **Adhere to the 10-minute rule.**

When a task seems overwhelming, only tell yourself that you will only work on it for 10 minutes. Ten minutes should not be too intimidating. More often than not, you will end up doing 10 minutes. It is the initial process of getting started that is the hardest to overcome.

8. **Use the Pomodoro technique.**

The Pomodoro technique is a time management method developed by Francesco Crillo. To use this technique, you will set a timer for 25 minutes and keep working on the task at hand until the timer goes off. This enables you to work without any distractions for the allotted time. Take a break when the timer goes off. Then do it all again.

9. **Misery loves company.**

Try to find another co-worker who has something they need to do and make a bargain - you will help them stay focussed (or help them finish their task) if they do the same for you. You can offer this in small, 30 minute chunks of time since so often, it's the initial momentum where we need the most help and having someone else's focus added to yours may be just the kick in the pants you need to take the first steps. Even if your work friend is not a procrastinator, they may appreciate being kept company on an otherwise dreary task!

10. **Prioritize your responsibilities and tasks.**

Make a list of everything you would like to accomplish and its degree of importance.

Write it all down in a list. Then color code or rank the tasks that require immediate energy and attention. You can also push back the tasks that are not urgent so you are able to prioritize the ones that have the shortest deadline.

11. **Delegate when you can.**

    Focus on the tasks that you personally need to complete and what responsibilities you are able to delegate to others. Delegating can help to establish and build professional relationships with your team members or colleagues. It can also free up more time for you to finish the projects that you personally need to complete.

12. **Think outside the box.**

    Give yourself a soft deadline before the actual deadline. Work ahead as much as you can. Figure out a system that works for you, then stick to it. One example is an internet-based productivity tool like *RescueTime* or *Leechblock*, both of which can help you decrease your distractions and stay on tasks with frequent prompts.

13. **Write it down.**

    Organize your tasks by when you need to have them done. You can even color code everything you need to accomplish. Consider using an organization app or online calendar that gives you reminders and notifications about the things you need to do. A great way to feel motivated and accomplished is to cross off items that you have completed.

14. Get a task-master.

Find someone else to push you and make sure you stop procrastinating, especially when you find it difficult to get yourself going. Enlist the help of a family member or co-worker. Tell your task-master to be hard on you and not as forgiving as you are to yourself.

15. Put public pressure on yourself.

The strong power that a deadline has is only multiplied when you combine it with public pressure. For instance, you are more likely to bust your butt in order to finish a project when your boss or other group of people expect it to be done by a certain time. For the tasks you need to complete that don't have any public pressure, create some yourself. Email someone and promise to finish your task by a certain deadline. Ask them to check on you to make sure you completed the task when the deadline arises.

Chapter 5: 14 Hacks to Overcome Procrastination at Home

Procrastination can <u>incur</u> stress that *could* have been completely avoided with motivation, time management, and planning. Oftentimes, the root of procrastination is found at the intersection of *feeling overwhelmed about the task at hand* **and** *having anxiety about the outcome of the finished project*. This is even more common when you are balancing multiple tasks and responsibilities at once.

In this chapter, we are going to look at 14 hacks to overcome procrastination at home. While all of the hacks listed in this book are an excellent place to begin, the ones listed in this chapter will be extremely beneficial if you are struggling with procrastination at home.

1. **Structured procrastination.**

    The idea behind structured procrastination is to put your most important task at the very top of your to-do list. Make sure this is a task with a deadline that is flexible and can be pushed back. Then put other important tasks right below the first one. As more important tasks come along, add them to the top of your list.

2. **Prepare yourself.**

    Once we prepare for a task it becomes much easier to get started. Clear away the distractions, get your tools ready, gather all of your research, get in the work zone with your cup of coffee, and get started.

3. **Track your time.**

    You will be better able to manage your time after you see just how much of it you are actually wasting. Track it by doing a time log, even if you only do it for one day. It will be enlightening. You will become more aware of what you are spending your time doing, and what your time-wasters are. You should be able to get your procrastination under control after you realize how much of your time has been unproductive.

4. **Stop trying to multitask.**

    Multitasking is a fatally deceptive addiction, no matter how attractive or trendy it seems. It is a myth that multitasking makes you more productive. You are not able to achieve more by trying to do several things at once. Don't even try to multitask.

5. **Try the procrastination dash.**

    This is basically a short burst of focused work. It can be as short as a minute. It is designed to get you out of procrastination mode. Set the timer on your phone for one to five minutes and perform a task you have been dreading - but only for that period of time. Do that once a day and watch your progress grow.

6. **Form a "Do it now" habit.**

Procrastination is simply a bad habit. Adopting a "Do it now" mentality will help you kick procrastination's butt. While this will require concentrated effort for 30 days, it will come naturally after that. Hang up a "Do it now" sign somewhere you will see everyday so you don't forget your new mindset.

7. **Remove distractions.**

Do you want to get more done by working distraction-free? Temporarily silence everything that has a continuous feed. Turn your phone to Do Not Disturb for an hour, silence your social media accounts and email on your computer, and enjoy focusing on the task at hand.

8. **Consider not doing it.**

Perhaps the task is something you shouldn't do, especially if you are really dreading it. While this is not always a valid option, some tasks are not absolutely necessary. After putting off the task for long enough, it may no longer be necessary to complete it by the time you get around to doing it. For example, misplacing your ID card at work and needing to ask for a new one is a task that might be postponed if waiting causes the lost ID card to turn up in a coat pocket!

9. **Start working on it now.**

Whatever it is, you must get started on it now. Don't ever wait for a better circumstance or to be in a better mood to get started. No one is guaranteed they have a future. New body cells are being created all the time because your cells are dying. In fact, even your own brain treats your future self as a complete stranger. These are all reasons why it is so important to get started *now.*

10. Try a mindfulness-based exercise.

It can help to observe the present moment without judgment, anxiety, or fear. You will find it easy to start working on a new project when your anxiety about the present is gone. Mindfulness can help you overcome procrastination by paring down your instant gratification urges regulated by the brain's limbic system. Some mindfulness techniques include meditation and grounding exercises. These are helpful in addressing your anxious thoughts and replacing them in a healthy way. You will be able to provide more, thoughtfully with intention, when you are able to calm your racing thoughts.

11. Define the outcome you want.

Consider the big picture aspect of the task or responsibility in front of you. What results do you expect? What is your endgame? Why does the task need to be accomplished? Does it help you professionally or personally?

Understanding what you want can help you act in a more systematic and focused way.

12. **Identify what makes you the most productive.**

    Do you find you often have new ideas after taking a nap? Do you have a favorite song that gives you inspiration? Do you do better when you draw out an outline before getting started? Figure out whatever helps you to be more productive and integrate these practices into your regular work schedule on a consistent basis. You can be more productive when you do work that you are passionate about. You will begin to feel more positive and energized.

13. **Acknowledge the problem.**

    The first step is understanding that it is you who is subverting your own plans. You must be able to recognize and admit that you have a problem with delaying things needlessly and deliberately.

14. **Be honest with yourself.**

    You must be realistic about the time that you can allot to tasks, without stressing out and spreading yourself too thin. Set some boundaries around the responsibilities and tasks that you commit to. Give yourself permission to make decisions that are in alignment with your aspirations and goals.

Chapter 6: 18 Hacks to Overcome Procrastination in Your Personal Life

The first thing to remember is that procrastination is a voluntary activity, meaning you do it on purpose. Procrastination is not something that happens by chance. In fact, it can be defined as an intentional delay in taking action.

Procrastination is something that even the most punctual and well-organized people will fall victim to one time or another. Think about the last time you found yourself watching TV or scrolling through social media when you should have been working on your homework instead. Procrastination can have a detrimental impact on your life in many different areas.

Procrastinators believe that time is against them and they have to figure out how to outpace it. Many procrastinators are perfectionists who can't finish the project until they are able to do it perfectly.

In this chapter, we are going to look at 18 hacks to overcome procrastination in your personal life. If you don't take action, all of the best hacks in the world will be unable to make you get over your procrastination. These hacks won't ever work unless you put them to work. Even if you are telling yourself that these won't work for you, it is important that you give these hacks a fair shot and keep an open mind.

1. Be more self-aware.

If you want to replace procrastination with more productive behaviors, you must first identify and understand your procrastination process. You need to look for similar patterns in the types of tasks that you typically put off or avoid. An example would be avoiding complicated tasks by excessively checking your email. You should understand that those tasks take more effort and be able to schedule them for when you are most productive. You can work on getting those challenging tasks out of the way first, after you are fully able to acknowledge your process for what it is.

2. Just get started.

Make a point to focus on the task at hand for 30 minutes without distraction or interruption, even when you feel the need to procrastinate. You can even set a timer if needed. Many people agree that once they are in the middle of working on a project they are more likely to want to complete it. In this way, you will be further along than you would have been if you had not started at all, even if you did end up taking that break after the half-hour.

3. Accept imperfection.

Perfectionists will procrastinate because they see their projects as more difficult than they should be. Learn to accept your imperfections instead of setting yourself up to be intimidated from the beginning. For example, jot down whatever first comes to mind when you are writing an important presentation and view it as a rough draft. You can go over it later in order to edit and clean it up. You will likely have more energy to sustain yourself through the rest of the workday when you free yourself from unreachable expectations. You may even begin to enjoy the projects you once procrastinated on.

Here's an example. When I write my books, I don't stress about the first draft. I just start writing and allow myself plenty of slack as my fingers fly across the keyboard. Getting a first draft is my only goal.

If your goal is to mop the floor and you know you need to sweep the floor before you mop it, just do the sweeping. When you see how nice it looks, you are likely to want to keep going and make it really nice by mopping.

4. **Focus on short-term goals and gains.**

An effective way to avoid procrastination is to break up big tasks into smaller ones. You could even throw around the idea for your company to have more minor check-ins and deadlines to keep everyone on task. Even if you are unable to change the structure of your deadlines, you can still ask yourself what you want to gain in the short term.

For example, how would you benefit from working on a project first thing in the morning instead of waiting to begin after lunch? You could have a more enjoyable lunch break because you made progress on your goals and you may not even feel rushed to get everything done by the end of the day. You may also begin to feel less overwhelmed when you break tasks up into smaller ones. For example, if you are writing a book you should first start with the outline and then identify each chapter. Rather than writing the entire first chapter, you can break it up into smaller sections and commit yourself to finishing one segment at a time. You may feel more empowered when you apply this technique to all of your projects and tasks.

When I make a list, the first thing I like to do is write "Make List" and then cross it off. It may seem silly, but in reality, once I've made the list, that's one less thing I have to do that day and I feel accomplished right out of the gate.

5. **Be realistic.**

Make sure to give yourself plenty of time to work on each project, especially because procrastination can come from inaccurately gauging how much time you will have. Being realistic also means that you understand your peak productivity times. Some people work better first thing in the morning, while others work best in the evening. You will be able to work more productively when you begin to understand how much time you need to complete the task and schedule time to work during your peak hours.

6. **Rephrase your internal dialogue.**

    You will feel like you have no choice if you tell yourself you need or have to work on your project. This kind of self-talk will only make you feel disempowered. Say, "I choose to do this" rather than "I have to". When you use more positive language, you can believe that you are in complete control and own the assignment. Say, "I can accomplish this" the next time you are feeling overwhelmed and facing a challenging task and see how much it empowers you.

7. **Optimize your environment.**

    Reevaluating your environment is one of the best things you can do to overcome procrastination. For example, you can easily be distracted from your task when you are surrounded by clutter. You can reduce your stress and boost your productivity simply by creating your ideal work environment. It is important to work in a comfortable and clean space with lots of natural light. You can also wear noise-canceling headphones if you are easily distracted by others, such as your co-workers. You can easily boost your productivity when you create a pleasant and distraction-free environment.

8. **Find an accountability partner.**

It is often easier to overcome procrastination and laziness when you enlist the help of someone. You can establish deadlines and stick to them when you have a good accountability partner. This can be anyone who can bring in an outsider's perspective and help you to remain focused, such as a co-worker, boss, friend, or client. Make sure you connect with your accountability partner at least once a week to discuss your upcoming schedules and everything you need to accomplish. Reach out to your partner when you find yourself procrastinating and tell them why you are struggling. A good accountability partner will be able to encourage you to reevaluate your approach so you are able to get back to your project.

9. **Reward productivity.**

If you complete the task you set out to do, without procrastinating, reward yourself. For example, only allow yourself that second cup of coffee after you have finished the project you are currently working on. You could also create a new habit of keeping your phone turned off until you work for a specific allotted time, and then reward yourself with spending some time on social media after your goals are completed.   There are two benefits to this: 1) it makes the process more enjoyable, which is important as you are more likely to do the task, and 2) it makes you look forward to completing the task, so you can earn the reward you set for yourself.

10. **Recognize the onset of procrastination.**

    Pay attention to when thoughts of procrastination begin to appear in your mind, especially as you are crossing off items on your to-do list. You should be able to recognize when you are about to procrastinate, especially if you find yourself thinking "I'll have time to work on this later" or "I don't feel like doing this right now". Don't give in when you are tempted to procrastinate. Force yourself to spend a little bit of time working on the task. You will find that it is easier to complete the task after you have begun.

11. **Overcome your fears.**

    If you give some thought to what can happen, you will be able to get your fears under control and even find ways to overcome them. Ask yourself what fears are blocking you from completing the task at hand. Fear of not being good enough? Or fear of failure? Think of the worst thing that could possibly happen and how bad it would be. It's often not near as bad as you have created it to be in your head.

12. **Change to an abundance mentality.**

    Rather than focusing on the obstacles or difficulties and problems with completing the task, consider the opportunities and possibilities presented. By thinking of it this way and contemplating the benefits and rewards that come from completing the task, you are more likely to want to start in the first place.

13. **Stop overthinking it.**

You must not allow yourself to over analyze or over think. You can't worry about how your final task will look or how you will be able to get through all of the steps. All overthinking does is tear down your willpower and wear you out.

14. **Celebrate the small wins.**

No matter how small your accomplishments are, make sure to acknowledge when you complete a task or project. You can feel more optimistic and positive about the future by taking inventory of what you have already completed. This can also increase your motivation. Praise yourself for the effort that you have made towards your end goal, and then be proud of yourself.

15. **Consider the impact on your health.**

Procrastination can lead to an increase in stress, thereby increasing the possibility of high blood pressure, and can result in a detrimental effect on your cardiovascular health. On the other hand, you will have increased energy and motivation when you make healthy lifestyle choices. One of the first steps in committing to a healthier way of life is to consult with a nutritionist on ways to integrate healthy options into your daily routine.

16. **Procrascipline.**

    Procrascipline is the love child of procrastination and discipline. The first rule of procrascipline is that you are not allowed to ignore the task. The second rule is that you must put it on a list you will look at throughout the day. The third rule is that you must communicate your progress (or lack thereof) to others. Don't procrastinate in doing the third step. You will be surprised that these three little rules truly work!

17. **Make it interesting.**

    Make the task or project interesting. One way you can do this is to turn the most boring parts of your project into a game you will enjoy. Ask your coach or professor for ideas on how to make it more interesting for you.

18. **Don't try to be a last-minute hero.**

    It is a lie to tell yourself that you work better under pressure. All of the jobs that were finished at the last minute in your past experiences were the result of not having them done when you had enough time, and not because you were given that small amount of time.

Conclusion

Procrastination is defined as putting off tasks either until the last minute or past their deadline. Some researchers go even further and say procrastination is a form of self-regulation failure that is characterized by the irrational delay of tasks despite any potentially negative consequences. Procrastination is a complex behavior that is rooted in multiple causes, including:

- Disinterest
- External stress
- Perfectionism
- Feeling overwhelmed
- Laxness
- Need for time-management techniques
- Inexperience

While everyone procrastinates from time to time, ADHD procrastination is a totally different thing. It is much more extreme, more regular, more damaging, harder to control, and paired with other symptoms. For people with ADHD, procrastination often occurs repeatedly and causes real problems at work, home, or in your personal life. Even if you recognize that procrastination is what is causing these problems, you likely feel as if it is out of your control to break the pattern.

In many cases, ADHD symptoms could happen to anyone. When multiple types of these behaviors occur repeatedly and cause serious problems, you might be suffering from ADHD. Therefore, procrastination itself does not necessarily suggest ADHD. Rather, it does raise questions when it is combined with other ADHD-related behaviors.

When we started with the four types of procrastinators, you probably saw yourself in one of them. Then when we examined the link between procrastination and ADHD, you hopefully began to forgive yourself for behavior that used to cause you distress. There is a *real and complex* relationship between procrastination and ADHD. While there is no direct link between the two, some of the ADHD symptoms can lead to procrastination. Everyone has a natural tendency to procrastinate occasionally. Many of us put off tasks we don't want to do until "later". **Sometimes** we set aside tasks because we are waiting until we have more energy to tackle them on a new day. Other days we simply set aside tasks until we are less overwhelmed with the noise in our heads.

The biggest problem for those with ADHD is that if their procrastination happens again and again, it becomes known as *chronic procrastination*. This then leads to severe problems at work, home, and even in your personal life. Even though many with ADHD can admit that their procrastination is significant and causing ongoing issues, they will find it challenging to break the pattern.

When you took the three minute procrastination challenge, you immediately got to do something about your procrastination tendencies. The only rules were that you actually got started on an important task, *without* procrastinating. Hopefully, you used one or more of the five in this chapter to help you get started in your new way of life.

The next three chapters went over other tips to overcome procrastination at work, home, and in your personal life. We started with hacks to overcome procrastination at work. Some of the hacks listed in this chapter suggested that you:

- Schedule non-negotiable windows of time
- Eliminate distractions
- Set a deadline
- Love your work
- Do your most important task first

When we jumped into hacks to overcome procrastination at home, you may recall some of the hacks listed in this chapter included:

- Prepare yourself
- Track your time
- Stop trying to multitask
- Remove social media distractions
- Consider not doing it

Finally, we talked about hacks to eliminate procrastination in your personal life. Some of the hacks listed in this chapter included advice on how you can:

- Be more self-aware
- Just get started
- Accept imperfection
- Focus on short-term goals and gains
- Rephrase your internal dialogue

While not everyone who procrastinates suffers from ADHD, you now know the complex relationship between the two. Procrastination is just one of several severe symptoms of ADHD. Many who procrastinate may not have ADHD unless there are other related behaviors.

You also now know 47 different hacks added to your toolbox to overcome procrastination in many areas of your life. You also have the success under your belt now because you *are* capable of conquering procrastination – you proved it when you successfully followed the three minute procrastination challenge. But don't stop there! The best thing you can do is to put the other procrastination hacks to good use – now. You don't have to use all of the hacks listed in this book. Find a few that work for you and start there.

The most important thing is that you find somewhere to start, in order to once and for all, overcome procrastination.

ADHD Time Blindness:
27 Hacks to Combat Time Blindness

Kristen Thrasher

Table of Contents

Introduction
Chapter 1: What is Time Blindness?
Chapter 2: How Time Blindness Really Feels
Chapter 3: Time Blindness Self-Test
Chapter 4: 9 Common Questions and Answers
Chapter 5: 27 Time Blindness Hacks
Conclusion

Introduction

Adult *attention-deficit/hyperactivity disorder (ADHD)* is a mental health disorder that causes a combination of persistent problems, such as difficulty paying attention, impulsiveness and hyperactivity, although some adults present without the hyperactivity and simply find it extremely difficult to focus. Adult ADHD can lead to poor school and/or work performance, unstable relationships, low self-esteem, and other issues, not the *least* of which is *time blindness*. *

Even though it is formerly known as *adult ADHD,* symptoms start in early childhood and then *continue on* through adulthood. However, in some cases it is not fully recognized or diagnosed until *adulthood*. There *are* <u>certain</u> symptoms that will <u>decrease</u> with adulthood, such as hyperactivity. However, there are several symptoms that persist well into adulthood, including restlessness, impulsiveness, difficulty paying attention, and time blindness. *

The term "time blindness" was coined specifically for ADHD in young adults in the 2001 paper: *Time perception and reproduction in young adults with attention deficit hyperactivity disorder.* Time blindness is defined as the inability to accurately sense the passing of time. It is important to note that rather than an intentional disregard for time, time blindness is a sensory issue that can cause nearly every aspect of your life to be more difficult than someone who has a good sense of the passage of time.

People with time blindness are unable to accurately measure time or even recall when certain memories took place. While anyone can experience time blindness on occasion (of course), it is a common symptom in people diagnosed with neurodevelopmental disorders, such as ADHD and autism.*

While all people have varying levels of time awareness, even if they do not have ADHD, experts believe there are many people with ADHD who suffer from time blindness, and therefore, have trouble with their awareness of the passing of time. Time awareness is your ability to assess when the timing of something is going to affect your life.

Time blindness affects the past, present, and future, and can even be explained as so. Time blindness in the past creates issues in terms of not knowing how long ago a specific event has happened. For example, your brain will know the circumstance occurred, but you won't have any clue how long ago it happened. There is no differentiation in your mind.

Time blindness in the present can make it difficult for you to judge how long an activity is going to take. It's also hard to adhere to deadlines. For example, because someone with time blindness has so much trouble being realistic about their time and planning well, they are not able to stick to deadlines without assistance.

Finally, time blindness in the future causes people trouble in terms of making plans. It comes down to your judgment of the passage of time. For example, it becomes hard to plan an activity because you have a less firm grip on what is required to plan and execute future events, such as a wedding six months in the future.

The goal of this book is to make you more aware of what time blindness is. Some people believe time blindness is a made-up condition to excuse bad behavior, but that isn't true. Time blindness is a real condition that generally goes hand-in-hand with ADHD, and there are many things you can do *now* to combat the symptoms and go on to live your best life!

Chapter 1: What is ADHD Time Blindness?

Neurotypical people will wonder what is so difficult about looking at your watch or the clock sitting on your desk. They wonder how you didn't realize you didn't have time to go to the store and still make it on time for your date. Or they will wonder how you could not know how long it takes to get ready for work in the morning (considering you do it every day), causing you to be late – every day! For people who do not suffer from this affliction, it's utterly baffling.

Time blindness makes even these most basic skills extremely difficult, if not downright impossible to master. In fact, time blindness causes a plethora of screw-ups, kills one's self-esteem, exacerbates one's emotional volatility, devastates otherwise stable relationships, and even puts you in danger of seriously harming yourself.

Because the human body senses time in a similar way that it senses sound, taste, and light, as well as other elements, a typical human brain can map out a reasonably accurate sense of what time of day it is, how much time there is before an upcoming event, and how much time has passed based on a mix of both external and internal cues or stimuli. However, this time perception is disrupted for people with ADHD, resulting in a symptom we call time blindness.

Those who suffer from time blindness struggle with seemingly trivial tasks, such as planning events a few weeks in advance, because it is so difficult for them to imagine very far into the future. Time management is a component of *executive functioning*, which is the part of your brain responsible for regulating and directing emotions, behaviors, and thoughts. It involves the ability to perceive the rate at which time passes, knowing what time it is, and how much time is left to complete a particular task or activity.

While still not fully understood, scalar expectancy theory (SET) is currently the most widely accepted framework for time perception among researchers. SET describes time perception as a type of internal clock that is measured out in pulse rates. It is nearly impossible for most people to estimate with any sort of accuracy when one minute has passed because a person's brain knows roughly how many times their heart is supposed to beat per minute; therefore, a person will intuitively start to feel as if the minute is almost up once that number of beats is near.

The brain then takes this pulse information and combines it with other sensory outputs, such as temperature changes or brightness levels in their environment, to form an overall picture of where they are in time, as well as how fast they are moving through time.

Time blindness is what happens when this process is either defective or disrupted, which leads

to a variety of issues, improperly labeled *poor time management*. They include:
- Constantly losing track of time, especially during transitions
- Chronically arriving late or missing deadlines, even for things you are excited about
- Feeling as if time is slipping away
- Overestimating or underestimating how much time has passed, how much time is left before an anticipated event, or even how long a particular task will take
- Difficulty sticking to a schedule, or making a realistic schedule in the first place

Because distractions tend to be a huge barrier for experiencing one's life as desired, it is inaccurate to say that people affected by time blindness only live in the present. Time blindness can also show up in other, albeit more subtle, areas. Some other issues of time blindness can include:
- Difficulty regulating the speed of movement, such as trying to make oneself walk slower
- Slow reaction or response times, such as putting one's hand up too late to catch a ball
- Procrastination
- Boredom
- Impulsivity
- Chronic tardiness (such as being unable to stay organized at school, home, or work)
- Intentions and results that don't always align

- Struggling to complete work or school assignments
- Being misjudged as lazy
- Feeling inadequate or like you're a constant disappointment to others
- Putting things off, such as doctor's appointments
- Being late paying bills and harming your credit rating even though you had the money to pay the bills
- Difficulty estimating how long ago a specific event happened, like when answering simple questions such as "When did you last go on vacation?" or "When did you eat lunch?"

There are three different time-related domains of the brain that are equally impacted by ADHD: temporal foresight, perceptual timing, and motor timing. We know there is a strong association between undesirable behavioral outcomes, such as inattention and impulsivity (which are the very basis of an ADHD diagnosis), and difficulty with managing time.

Someone who has trouble concentrating can also experience other issues including an inability to meet expectations or demands at both home and work. Adults with ADHD-related time blindness can feel inadequacy, shame, and guilt due to bosses or partners becoming frustrated by their chronic loss of productivity.

The bottom line is, a person who has a misjudgement of time due to their time blindness has a *sensory issue*, and is not making a bad independent choice on their own.

While time blindness can range from minor to significant in terms of how much it affects you, all cases are difficult for sufferers. However, people are able to make positive changes with a combination of acceptance, solution-focused treatment, and cognitive-behavioral therapy. It is extremely helpful to work with a mental health professional, even if only on a short-term basis, especially regarding acquiring new skills and mapping out a plan for change.

However frustrating it may be, time blindness is treatable with both behavioral and cognitive approaches. It is important to balance solutions with the validation that having ADHD is *not* a choice that any person makes - after all, why *would* they?

Chapter 2: How Time Blindness Really Feels

Time blindness feels like you are suspended in an eternal present. An example would be you forgetting to set a timer, putting a pot of water on to boil and leaving the kitchen for "five minutes", only to come back hours later to find an empty pot and that all the water has evaporated.

Another good example is when you check the clock at 7:05, go back to reading your book for "a bit", and after what honestly feels like a few minutes to you, you look back at the clock only to see that it is now 11:35.

The reason people with time blindness fail to meet deadlines is because they have no idea how to accurately plan things in a way that ensures it is completed by the deadline.

Research has found that an increase in dopamine levels (monetary rewards and prescription stimulants in this case) were able to improve time perception in participants with ADHD.

So what does all of this mean? It means that time blindness in ADHD tends to be a combination of insufficient dopamine levels to trigger an intentional or conscious tracking of time and the brain failing to passively or unconsciously interpret sensory input, such as light levels, pulse rate, and temperature changes, as indicators of time passing.

One of the biggest downsides to time blindness is that it hurts your relationship with yourself, as well as others. Because time management has deep ties to respect and love, those who we are close to feel let down when our time blindness gets the best of us. For example, say you promise to meet your significant other for dinner at 7:00, but you show up an hour late instead. How would your date feel? Especially after making excuses to the server and perhaps even ordering a single glass of wine at a table set for two.

Showing up late to dates, doctor's appointments, work, and family functions sends the message that you value the person you are meeting less than whatever made you late, even though that's not the case. You likely just lost track of time, like a dog who slipped off its leash when you weren't looking! In fact, the person you left waiting most likely feels as if they will never be as important as anything else in your life. However, people with ADHD know that this is not true.

For ADHD sufferers, their actions and intentions do not align with who they really are. They experience an astonishing difference between the self they know and their actions. They are subjected to harsh criticism by friends, family, employers, and even their own children! Being called "flakey" is probably one of the gentler descriptives they grow accustomed to over time as they become desensitized to constantly apologizing and approaching every transaction from a place of weakness due to lack of punctuality.

In our society, we start teaching time management to kids at an early age. In fact, many five-year-olds recognize when it's time to stop one activity to move on to the next one. With that in mind, imagine how heartbreaking it is for an adult with time blindness to fail at this simple life skill. It can be easy for us to forget these skills must be taught; they do not come naturally.

Those with ADHD have an extremely difficult time learning time management. What's worse, someone with untreated or undiagnosed ADHD may not be able to learn any time management skills, and find it difficult to manage relationships as a result. Remember, failure in managing time doesn't mean the person is irresponsible; rather, it means they are struggling with a problem they lack the tools to fix.

While it appears to everyone else that a person with time blindness doesn't care, this is not only untrue, it is also hurtful to the victim of time blindness.

One way for people who have never experienced time blindness to think about the condition is to realize that time blindness is as much of a "choice" as color blindness is. People who are colorblind cannot perceive differences between certain hues, even though they know differences exist and that other people can differentiate between them. Likewise, those who are time blind may know they need to leave work in time to meet their significant other for dinner, or that they should check the clock more often so they do not lose track of time. However, that knowledge doesn't help them when they forget to check the clock, or maybe that time even exists at all when they get on a roll. When they are unable to accurately perceive the passage of time, they are also unable to perceive their significant other waiting for them at a dinner table. They have a difficult time feeling the approach of a deadline as it closes in.

It is one thing to know a fact in your brain, such as, "I need to make sure I am on time for my dinner reservation", or "This flower garden is full of beautiful shades of pink and purple." However, it is quite another thing to experience these things at a sensory level. People wouldn't assume that a colorblind person doesn't care enough about distinguishing red from green, so they therefore shouldn't assume that a person suffering from ADHD doesn't care enough to manage their time properly.

Time blindness can also be dangerous. Not only can a faulty perception of time destroy our self-esteem and damage relationships, it also presents an immediate danger to the emotionally volatile person suffering from ADHD.

One harmful aspect is the tendency to hyperfocus, which is the "in the zone" state that many praise as a so-called ADHD superpower. Hyperfocusing is disruptive to your sense of time, and while it does occur with activities, it can also occur with your emotions as well.

Your inability to perceive time apart from the present moment fans the flames of emotional hyperfocus, which may seem charming when the person can only see the good or the excitement in the current moment. When the person is happy, they are all in, 100% happy. However, the opposite is also true. A negative event can easily trigger intense and even frightening emotions. In fact, many people with time blindness risk losing sight of their worth in relationships, or worse, life in general.

It would be irresponsible to ignore the emotional impact of time blindness because a simple mistake can lead to inescapable acts of self-sabotage, the desire to escape the bad feelings that present themselves, and obsessive thoughts of self-harm for a person suffering from ADHD. These can easily manifest in behaviors like drinking, overeating, compulsive shopping, gambling, or even a combination of escapism behaviors that only lead to more problems, also known as "the crutch that cripples".

It is true that many people with time blindness suffer greatly for their mistakes. In fact, your inaccurate perception of time is the source of great misunderstandings and painful experiences.

Chapter 3: Time Blindness Self-Test

How many times have you thought to yourself, "I would love to do that, but I just don't have the time"? We know that time is the great equalizer of life. It is the one thing every person has in common. Everyone has the same 24 hours in a day, no more and no less, regardless of how rich or how poor one may be.

Thanks to our digital world, time has become distorted by a plethora of new time-sucks like text messaging, social media, and a seemingly endless supply of visual and or written online content. These time leeches shine a spotlight on a new generation of time blind people. Those who never realized they were afflicted before they sat down to "check out Instagram for a minute" and lost two hours of their life. Since many of the solutions to the time blindness problem are in digital form, an irony springs into existence about what solutions there are for those who struggle.

Some digital aids help boost productivity, such as time management websites or apps. However, for those who enslave themselves to their laptop, tablet, or smartphone, these tools can create the opposite effect. Sometimes you need to take your search for productivity offline, as sometimes the barest basics can help you manage your time the best.

The self-test in this chapter will help you better understand what it feels like to be time blind. All you need is twenty minutes of uninterrupted time and your smartphone. You probably need this test more than anyone if you don't feel as if you even have twenty minutes to take this test. You may pause this recording at any time. There are two parts to this self-test, part A and part B.

1. The first of four steps in Part A is to set your phone's timer to ten minutes. (5)
2. For the second step in Part A, lay your phone face down so you cannot see the time running out.
3. Step three in Part A is to make sure not to look at any clocks elsewhere.
4. Finally step four in Part A - go do as many small tasks around your residence that you feel you can fit into the allotted time. Don't spend any of your time planning what tasks you are going to accomplish. Simply do the tasks as you identify them, and keep working until the timer goes off.

After the timer goes off, now comes Part B of the test.

1. Step One in Part B is to start by setting the timer on your phone for another 10 minutes.
2. Step two in Part B, make sure not to put your phone down this time.
3. Step three in Part B is to do whatever you would like. For example, text a friend or scroll

through social media - just don't wait for the timer to go off or look at the ticking timer.

There are two different things you will notice after taking this time blindness test. First, let's talk about the time you spent doing things while your phone was laying face down. While this time likely felt more rushed because you knew you were up against a ticking timer, you were ultimately likely to get more done in that time than you thought you could in ten minutes. In fact, these ten minutes may even have felt like they were more productive. Even though you were anticipating the timer, you probably felt more energized after it sounded.

Next, let's talk about the time that you spent on your phone. It's highly likely that when the timer sounded, it caught you off guard. It is also likely that this second 10 minute segment seemed to *fly* by, almost causing you to question whether it was really 10 minutes or not. This is a perfect representation of what time blindness feels like.

This test represents how you perceive tasks under two different sets of circumstances. In fact, what you just experienced is the time equivalent of the age-old riddle "What weighs more? A ton of bricks, or a ton of feathers?" When we have the ability to focus on the tasks at hand, our brain feels that since we are moving feathers, and since the task was to move as many feathers as possible in the amount of time allotted, the logical solution is to try to move more feathers for the best results, and even find ways to move more feathers at once. This is how your brain is wired, to seek an effective and efficient output of energy for maximum return.

However, the nature of approaching tasks is completely different. Remember that both weigh exactly a ton, whether it's a ton of bricks or a ton of feathers. Therefore in the second scenario where you spent 10 minutes on your phone, your phone plays the role of gravity. Ultimately, your phone was the force that differentiated between the difficulty of lifting a brick relative to lifting a feather.

Your phone distorts how you expend energy and perceive time, which can cause certain tasks to feel more laborious than others. In fact, you are aware of a timeline even without your phone, but you don't sit and obsess over it. By sheer human nature, this pushes you into greater productivity.

On the other hand, the distortion of time can also muddle how you view tasks as you become hyper-aware of the passage of time, especially in relation to the lack of tasks achieved in a certain amount of time. Your brain has been rewired to accept a state where your attention is fully engaged by stimulus on your phone, even though you are not physically doing anything other than sitting there, staring at a small device. It is a known fact that the absence of physical exertion causes mental exhaustion, which leads to errors and physical exhaustion. xxx

A study performed by FSU in 2013 found that the probability of making an error increased by 23% after receiving a text message, and by 28% after receiving a phone call. This is evidence that while your phone can physically exhaust you in the same way that a comparable amount of time spent working can, it can also cause you to be far less accurate with your work.

This also means that under ideal conditions, by not obsessively responding to every ding of your devices, you are not only capable of accomplishing more, but also able to experience a euphoric "high" from how many small tasks you were able to accomplish without interruption. Because of this, people can crave that good feeling and be even more empowered to stay *off* their phone in order to accomplish more tasks in a timely manner.

Let's take a moment to compare this to a workout where someone who works out starts off easy, then slowly builds up their workouts gradually over time. For the purpose of long-term gain and endurance, they will challenge their limits each time. The little test you took above works on the same psychological level. It is intended to recalibrate your internal clock to the *actual* time tasks require, rather than how many of us have built them up in our heads.

Chapter 4: 9 Common Questions and Answers

In this chapter, we are going to look at 9 of the most common questions and answers related to time blindness. While in no particular order, the questions and answers provided in this chapter should help you to form a better idea of how much time blindness truly affects you.

Some of the questions and answers in this chapter include how time blindness can turn your life into extremes, how to explain time blindness to your loved ones, some *benefits* to being time blind, what types of problems time blindness causes, and when you should turn to mental health professionals for help.

As you can see, there are a wide variety of questions and answers covered in this chapter alone. The goal is to help you fully understand how people are affected by time blindness. Ready? Let's get started.

1. **How does time blindness turn your life into extremes?**

    There are only two times for a time blind person: now and not now. That means the doctor's appointment you have next week, your cousin's wedding in a month, and that project you need to have finished three months from now are not on your radar. Because those are not *now*.

Due to the fallout from tasks that require great focus and preparation, people with time blindness can find their lives in extreme amounts of chaos. They continuously fall further behind on their future tasks because they are frequently putting out fires from their current disaster. To put it simply, they are reactive, not proactive. When a deadline slips, they are on it. Putting out fires becomes a way of life. As a result, life can feel like you're running on a hamster wheel, never really going anywhere or gaining any progress. Even though it feels like you're running at the highest speed possible. Everyone wants to feel like their hard work is paying off. However, people with time blindness feel like they're failing, even though they continue to work hard. But working hard isn't always the answer. Working smart can benefit you more than working hard when your hard work is barely keeping the fires out.

There are aspects of life that require being able to create and follow through with a plan. While time blindness may never go away, it is possible to learn skills in order to help maintain and control it.

2. How can you combat time blindness?

One of the very first steps in combating time blindness is to start mastering time instead of being its constant slave. It is not abnormal to find a tool or device, or even use technology, to help train your brain to better estimate the passage of time. Keep in mind that people with time blindness are not incapable of recognizing the passage of time, they just aren't "naturals". But just because you're not a natural swimmer, doesn't mean you cannot work hard and one day win the Olympics! Maybe you have no interest in winning the Olympics of time management, but wouldn't it be nice for once not to feel like you're constantly drowning? Acquiring this skill isn't the insurmountable task it might seem like.

Learning how to mark the passage of time is called *externalizing*. These specific tools are there to mark the passage of time, which is what your brain is having trouble doing on its own. We will dive much further into ways to combat time blindness in the next chapter, where we look at 27 specific time blindness hacks to help you better manage time.

3. **What are the negative consequences of time blindness?**

Time blindness has major repercussions in people's lives. Not showing up for work on time, being late for meetings, or keeping your significant other waiting a half hour for your dinner date are just a few examples. All of the above things happen when you are suffering from time blindness, and many people are too annoyed or frustrated to try to understand why this happens to their loved ones.

Time blindness to the untrained eye looks like a willful disregard of time for others, making employers or significant others especially unforgiving. Many people will even begin to exclude the person with time blindness from their plans and activities because they cannot properly understand how they can support them.

Many are quick to make rude comments about the time blind person's lateness and (justifiably) insult them by saying things such as, "I already know you are going to be late" or "I can't trust you to be on time". These and other insensitive remarks don't take into account that the most frustrated person is the one who is suffering from ADHD.

Many become so frustrated by the time blindness symptoms, they no longer see them as symptoms they have to deal with, but rather as a character flaw that personally offends them. It can cause serious damage to your relationships when people begin to take your time blindness personally.

4. **How can I explain time blindness to the people in my life?**

People are quick to reject explanations and demand you stop making excuses, especially when you bring up the fact that you have an actual condition which causes your issues with time. For some reason, when you explain your issues and give the reason, many assume it is just an excuse. For this reason, it's simpler to explain that you have *trouble estimating time* and leave out the ADHD diagnosis altogether. After all, it's the truth.

Instead of setting yourself up for an argument you are sure to lose, tell people that you have difficulty estimating how long something will take or that you become absorbed in projects easily causing you to lose track of time. Unless you feel that there is a reason why they should specifically know about the disorder itself, it is much easier to explain all of the symptoms without explaining the root cause. This is an excellent way to work around the whole "don't use ADHD as an excuse" pushback that people have heard time and again.

5. **Are there any benefits to being time blind?**

For every negative, you can also find a positive, even if it is hard to see. There are several benefits. Some examples include being able to lose yourself in a good book and forgetting the world for a bit. Or getting swept up by a project you feel passionate about. In fact, many people feel the most alive when they are operating out of the constraints of hours, minutes, and seconds.

Even though hyperfocus can cause you major havoc, it can also offer true happiness.

It's not always possible for neurotypical people to focus on something when they want to. While hyperfocus is not something you should rely on to get your tasks accomplished, because it can be so fickle, it can be a pleasant distraction when you are able to align it with your favorite interests.

6. **Is time blindness only linked with ADHD?**

   Experts are continuing to agree that this is rather unlikely. In fact, time blindness has also been linked with anxiety, depression, grief, sleep deprivation, and even the overuse of alcohol.

   Because these conditions can all dramatically affect your mental health and how you view the world, they will impact the executive function of your brain, which is a set of mental skills including self-control, flexible thinking, and a working memory.

   The more people know about time blindness and the more mental and physical health conditions that are linked to it, the more people are likely to be diagnosed with it - and understand it.

7. **How do I stop hyperfocus before it starts?**

   Because hyperfocus happens so naturally, you might not be able to help yourself most of the time. Once you get drawn into a task you love to hyperfocus on, it is not at all shocking that you are unable to tear yourself away.

It is best to try and stay away from the tasks you normally find yourself hyperfocusing on before you have to do something important so that you don't lose track of time. If you absolutely cannot stay away, you must make a firm commitment to yourself: give yourself a set amount of time and stop when you said you would.

Another good idea is to do the same tasks at the exact same time every day as repetition will produce a rhythm for your day that is simply unavoidable. It will help form the habit of you doing these same tasks within the same *time frame*. Just as with any other form of repetition, it will become easier to mark the passage of time when you perform a task over and over at the same time.

When you need to estimate the time it will take you to complete a task, always estimate based on the worst-case scenario. Many people with time blindness are guilty of estimating from the best-case scenario, or even leaving out steps it takes in order to complete the task at hand. Both of these can result in not allowing enough time for yourself to complete the task. For example, you might not be budgeting the amount of time you need to run back home after forgetting something on your way to work, or making a late start due to traffic, or any other worst-case scenario. You've driven three blocks from home and you think because it only took you a minute to get to where you are, you can run back home for a minute. Wrong. The minute to get home. The minute to go inside and get what you forgot. And heaven help you if you get distracted by something once you're back home. Another minute to get out and lock up, and the final minute to get back to that three blocks mark. If you hit red lights in those three blocks (worst case scenario), add another minute. Suddenly, one minute to "run home" has become five minutes!

There are any number of real-life worst-case scenarios that you may encounter, whereas most people with time blindness only budget for the exact amount of time it takes to get in their car and drive straight to work. Instead, make sure to always allow for the worst-case scenarios that are bound to pop up from time to time. Always allow some extra time, whatever the reason may be. It is critical to set alarms for when you need to start getting yourself together to leave, and another alarm for when you really need to leave the house, after adding in any additional time it might take you.

8. **What kind of problems does time blindness cause?**

Time blindness is an extremely troublesome symptom, especially because the entire world runs on time. You must show up everywhere on time, including if you have a job, take a class, or even want to go watch a movie at the theater. These are all common issues, but there are many other ways time blindness can affect you.

Time blindness not only affects your ability to be on time, but also your ability to estimate how much time a certain task or activity takes. In fact, many people struggling with time blindness must continue to estimate the duration of multiple tasks throughout the course of a day. Certain questions can make it hard for a person with time blindness to gauge, including "How long will a task take me?" or "How long will it take me to get ready to go out?" or "What is the length of the commute?"

Not only this, but we also live in an impatient world in which everyone expects us to have quick answers for the questions listed above. Many people will even become upset with people if their estimate is even the slightest bit off. It starts to feel like a lose-lose scenario. It can be very helpful when we explain our issues to the important people in our lives so they can better understand our challenges.

9. **When should you turn to a mental health professional for help?**

While it varies for every person, you should begin seeking help from a mental health professional when you begin feeling alone and isolated by symptoms, especially those closest to you. Another time to seek help is when you are having trouble with productivity at either school, home, or work. In fact, many people only begin seeking professional help when their boss, significant other, or close family member has made it known that they feel there is an underlying issue.

Before seeking professional assistance, it is crucial that you first learn the term neurodiverse. Being neurodiverse or neurodivergent means having a brain that works differently from the average or "neurotypical" person. Now that you know this, you will want to seek a neurodiverse-affirming therapist who has experience and understanding treating neurodiversity disorders. This can be done by searching for this skill through different providers, and then confirming through the initial consultation. Before deciding on a particular mental health professional, ask how they would go about treating symptoms of ADHD, especially your chief concern with regard to time blindness.

In addition to therapy, another great way to map out deficits and imbalances in a healthy and safe way, while also working towards desired stability, is family therapy. And finally, remember to ask your mental health professional about referrals for any additional testing or medication management.

Chapter 5: 27 Time Blindness Hacks

Having a good sense of time is a critical executive function that involves knowing what time it is, how quickly time is passing, and how much time is left before the next thing you need to do. Someone with time blindness is not aware of the ticking clock. Because of this, they struggle to use their time in the most effective way. In order to overcome the time blindness phenomenon, we must take a deeper dive and take a look at how people understand time.

One important concept in time management is known as the "time horizon", which is essentially how far you can look into the future to plan ahead. Your time horizon tops out at around one hour when you are a child. The more you age, the further away your time horizon becomes, so that the person is able to plan out the next year or two at a time.

Not all, but some who suffer from time blindness have a shorter time horizon than neurotypical people. In order for you to extend your time horizon, you need to become more aware of time.

In this chapter, we are going to look at ways you can use each and every hour of your day more effectively. It is difficult for someone with time blindness to realize when they are wasting time in the moment. However, there are basic keys to success, including staying aware of time and using it well. The hacks listed in this chapter are aimed at helping you become more productive and, in turn, will help you live your best life!

Before you begin going through the hacks, make sure to focus on identifying your areas of impact. Consider which areas of your life are being impacted the most due to time blindness. Some examples of this would be family, work, friends, or other social endeavors. After identifying the greatest areas of impact, you can map out your plans to ensure better time management skills. All of the hacks listed below can help, but you must first start by identifying the area of greatest impact and go from there.

1. **Allow for free time.**

    Make sure you do not schedule appointments back to back. If every second of the day is spoken for, your calendar will begin to feel crowded. You are more likely to follow your schedule when you allow for flexibility. Therefore, it is crucial to schedule chunks of free time along with everything else on your calendar.
2. **Encourage yourself throughout the day.**

    All people have highs and lows throughout the day. You can use these exact times to set up different feel-good messages to literally pop up on your phone right when you need them the most. For example, setting an hourly alarm with an encouraging message might include, "Challenge yourself to cross something off your to-do list right now," or "You are doing more than you are giving yourself credit for." These little reminders can help give you the little boost needed to stay on track.

3. **Set timers.**

    Make sure you set timers in advance, to avoid the risk of losing track of time. The timer will help pull you back to reality and remind you that you need to check the clock in order to finish the task at hand on time.

    One example would be to set a timer before you open social media to make sure you close the app within a reasonable time frame instead of getting lost for hours on end. Another example would be to never leave the kitchen when you are cooking without first setting a timer that will remind you to come back and check on the food. Remember to decide ahead of time how much time to allot to a certain task or activity, and then set the timer for that amount of time. This will prevent you from getting lost in what you are doing and losing track of time.

4. **Consciously track time.**

    It is important to take a few days to focus on how long it really takes you to do all of your daily tasks that repeat. Once you have accurate data to refer to, it can be easier to judge how long it takes you to do all of your daily tasks and activities. Start keeping a time log to determine where the time goes. Just like you budget your money, you may actually enjoy budgeting your time! Start timing yourself for tasks where you need an accurate perception of time. You can try using a time tracking app or creating a spreadsheet. Start by logging the time you start, including time for breaks. Then write down the time you finish the activity. This will become an invaluable resource in terms of planning out your daily schedule since it gives you a far more accurate idea of how long tasks really take.

5. **There's an app for that.**

    Activity Timer is a great tool for managing time. This app breaks your time into chunks so you can see what proportion is left without having to do any math. Another excellent choice is *Time Timer*. This app gives you a visual sense of both how much time has passed and how much time you have left. Other ones that work well are *30/30* and *StayOnTask*. Try several different apps or websites before settling on a final choice.

6. **Don't play the blame game.**

    There are many successful interventions and solutions that lessen the severity of your time blindness symptoms, no matter how debilitating it may seem. While it is natural to feel frustrated, be sure to give yourself the credit you deserve for trying to improve yourself by getting the help you need. Playing the blame game will not make anything any better, you will simply become more frustrated with yourself. As long as you are consciously making the effort to better yourself and become more aware of your time, then you deserve a pat on the back. xxx

7. **Plan for worst-case scenarios.**

It can be extremely helpful to deliberately figure out the worst-case scenarios for every situation. This will ensure that you allow yourself enough time to complete each task on time. One example would be a person who tends to underestimate how long it takes for them to get somewhere. Try doing the math slowly and always allow yourself as much breathing room as possible in case the worst-case scenario comes up. You will have a much better chance of arriving on time when you allow extra time for worst-case scenarios.

8. **Keep a clock in each room of your house.**

It will be much easier to track the passage of time when you have an abundance of clocks. Time expands and compresses in surprising ways for people with time blindness causing them to struggle with processing time. In fact, a shortened time horizon can cause difficulty planning events and projects. When a clock is readily available in every room, you will be able to keep track of the time, no matter what room you have ventured into. For example, if you need to be in the school pick up line to get your children by 3:00 and the worst-case scenario is that the terrible traffic will take you 45 minutes, make sure to round that up to an hour and decide to leave your house at 2:00, and no later.

9. **Get some sleep.**

Many people with time blindness struggle with waking up and preparing for their day. It's easy to see that morning problems are a result of leftover night problems. This means that a big part of a successful morning is going to bed on time and getting enough sleep. People cannot function well if they are exhausted due to lack of sleep. Force yourself to turn off the TV and put away your work. You will have a better routine when you go to bed at the same time every night, even on the weekends. If you have trouble sleeping, try using a sleep timer and allowing an audio book to read you to sleep. Or try a meditation YouTube video to lull you into a pleasant state of relaxation. People who live in a noisy environment (large cities, near a highway, train tracks, airport, etc) have reported success with noises all night long like the sound of waves from a white noise maker, or a black screen video of a thunderstorm. Constant sounds of nature trick your brain into sleeping soundly and prevent other noises from interfering in your sleep.

10. **Accountability Buddy.**
Someone with time blindness struggles with long-term planning which leads to missed deadlines, stress and financial problems. Because time management and planning doesn't come naturally to some people, it is important to make intentional and explicit long-term goals. Examples include breaking up projects into smaller goals and enlisting a coach or friend to give you some accountability. Make sure to consider where you want to be in a year, and then plan what you need to do to make those goals or dreams come true. Working backwards makes things easier. Just like a road trip, start with your destination, and figure out what it will take for you to arrive realistically at your destination, and go backward from there.
11. **Break up daunting tasks.**
Those with time blindness tend to freeze up, especially when faced with a large project or task. You see time moving, yet the task at hand becomes so daunting, you can't make yourself start whatever it is you need to be doing. The best plan is to break the final goal into smaller segments. One method is to start with the easiest and smallest task. An example can be found in your daily "getting ready" routine. Instead of thinking of it as, "I have to get ready for work", which can seem nearly impossible, try thinking of each little step to

getting ready, such as "I need to get dressed" and "I need to brush my teeth," and so on. In this way, you will be ready before you know it.

12. **Own your flaws.**

It goes without saying that most people are not happy or proud to have a neurodevelopmental disorder, or any mental health disorder for that matter. However, there are always ways you can lighten the load of your disorder, even without invalidating your experience. Find someone you can talk to. You are likely to find many similarities and be able to rest assured that you are not alone in your struggles with time blindness.

13. **Make your clocks work *for* you.**

There are multiple ways you can make the clock work for you. Some people have good results when they switch from digital clocks to analog clocks. Analog clocks allow you to see how much time you have left while the hand moves and the time physically shrinks. This is an excellent way to get a sense for the passage of time. Another example is to set your clocks a few minutes ahead, but make each clock a slightly different amount. For example, make the microwave clock 11 minutes fast while the bedroom clock is 9 minutes fast. Try not to use an easy number like 5, 10 or 15 because it's too easy for your brain to do the math! By never knowing exactly what time it is, you will be more likely to get the lead out and be less distracted. The shock value of time will hit you sooner which, in turn, gets you in gear more quickly.

14. Be aware of "time sucks".

It is important for you to refuse an activity that you do not have time for. Instead, focus on putting *your own needs first* in order to reduce stress, preserve your sanity, and make your life easier. A time suck is any activity that you become lost in. Time sucks are anything that distracts you to the point where you lose track of time when you are doing that activity. Some examples are social media, listening to music, or watching television. Making yourself aware of time sucks can be beneficial. It is also a good idea to give yourself limits before you ever even begin an activity in which you are certain to lose track of time.

15. Strategize your alarms.

An alarm is an effective and simple tool that can help make you more aware of the passage of time. An alarm will break into your consciousness and jolt you out of your current activity. You can set reminders with descriptions and/or alarms as a way to not only remind yourself what you need to be doing and when, but to also keep yourself motivated. You can even make your reminders both engaging and fun by calling out unhelpful behaviors and owning your triggers. An example of this would be a specific alarm that tells you "Adam, you really don't have time for this right now; put your phone down so you can stay on track."

You may find that one alarm is not enough and you need to set several. An example would be setting an alarm one half hour before you need to leave, then 15 minutes before you need to leave, and then immediately before you need to leave. Every extra alarm that you set multiplies the probability that you will make the transition at the proper time and not be late.

16. **Enlist the help of a coach.**

If you have tried setting alarms and found they are of no help, enlist the help of a coworker, friend, or spouse. You can ask your person of choice to call you at a specific time in order to remind you of where you need to be or what you are supposed to be doing when the alarm goes off. In extreme circumstances, they may even need to stay with you until you get moving.

17. **Mix it up.**

Instead of using the same generic beep for every alarm, try changing the alarm to different sounds in order to signify different things. For example, use one sound when it is time to get ready for an important event, and a different sound when it is time to take your medication. Varying alarms are harder to ignore and also more likely to get you on the right track.

18. **Reset your focus time.**

    Try changing the time that you associate with an event. For example, if you have to leave for work at 7:30, but your brain doesn't become motivated until it's already 8:30, you then enter crisis mode every morning. Instead, train your brain to focus on 7:00 as the time you need to start getting ready to leave the house. You can become more conscious of how long things take simply by changing the time you pay attention to the most.

19. **Include buffer time in your schedule - triple every estimate.**

    Because you may not be good at judging how long things take, you must factor in some buffer time. Buffer time is extra time you don't think you will need, but do. If you think it will take you 15 minutes to do an activity, try allowing 45 minutes. If you think it will take you an hour to complete a task, allow two hours, just in case. This will give you some wiggle room and prevent overloading your schedule, just in case you begin to get sidetracked at any time during the day, which is likely to happen. If you find yourself with "extra time", you can always reward yourself with some down time doing something you normally limit such as TV or social media.

20. **Listen to music.**

    Music has been proven to help many people focus for a longer amount of time, simply by listening to it. It is even more crucial for people with time blindness, as it has the added benefit of improving one's ability to perceive time. Background music may provide the emotional stimulation that is needed in order for your brain to kick its own time perception into gear. It may also provide an external cue for your brain to track time, even while you are focusing on other tasks altogether. You could also try using music instead of timers. For example, instead of setting a timer for one hour before you begin a new task or activity, try putting on an album or playlist that lasts for one hour instead. You can even make a variety of playlists ahead of time that vary in length so you will have them when you need them.

21. **Give yourself a hit (or two) of dopamine.**

    Increasing dopamine levels will likely help with time blindness, as it has been linked to dopamine deficiencies. Many of the cognitive issues that people with time blindness experience tend to also relate to low dopamine levels. The examples below are all excellent habits that can also help moderate your other ADHD symptoms. In order to build an enhancing dopamine routine, you can try including some or all of the following things

    - **Drink coffee:** Caffeine is a stimulant, just as other prescription medications for ADHD. Because of this, coffee will have

a similar effect, albeit much milder. Make sure to keep your daily intake of caffeine to less than 4 cups of coffee which is below 400 milligrams.
- **Exercise:** Exercise stimulates dopamine production.
- **Eat foods rich in vitamin B6:** B6 deficiency is associated with dopamine deficiencies. Some good sources of B6 include bananas, dark leafy greens, oranges, chickpeas, and fish.
- **Get out in the sunlight:** The sunlight stimulates neurotransmitters that can trigger dopamine release.

22. **Use a planner.**

While it may take a while to get used to the new habit, it can be invaluable to use a planner to record your projects and events. You can use a wide variety of tools, including a day planner, a calendar, or an online tool or app. However, the use of some sort of planner can prove to be critical for anyone with time blindness to help manage their shortened time horizon.

23. **Start with something easy.**

It is rewarding to cross off even one or two small tasks from your to-do list. This will help to increase a sense of effectiveness and purpose for your day. Take it one step at a time and don't forget about the little things you do accomplish. Praise yourself for trying to make improvements. Remember to pat yourself on the back for your solid efforts.

24. Start with the largest task.

While contrary to the previous hack, some people prefer to start with the hardest or most lengthy task first. This way, they know that the hardest part is behind them. After finishing the difficult task, the rest of their to-do list seems easier in comparison. This gives them motivation to keep going and complete the whole project.

25. Play the 5 Minute Game.

This game can be played anytime, anywhere. The idea is that you set a countdown timer on your phone for 5 minutes. Make sure before you begin that you have taken care of all your biological needs (bathroom, water, etc). You need 5 focussed and uninterrupted minutes. If your phone dings, ignore it. If you get a call, ignore it. Start the timer and focus on a task you normally dread. Maybe it's emptying the dishwasher. See how far you can get in 5 minutes. It might shock you to learn that you can put all the dishes away in less than 4 minutes! Maybe it's folding laundry or making a grocery list. Maybe it's cleaning your Inbox of junk mail. Maybe it's paying bills. The point is, after 5 minutes, you stop and reassess. Do you want to reset for another 5 minutes? Or do you want to stop and do something else? The point is that your brain starts to learn what 5 minutes feels like and you will see that you can get quite a bit accomplished in 5 minutes, probably far more than you ever imagined. Without interruptions, you can get tasks done that you normally dread doing!

26. **Allow time between appointments, aka, "The 50 Minute Hour".**

    Even a 10-15 minute gap between appointments or meetings can give you the opportunity to take coffee or snack breaks, use the restroom at your leisure and not feel pressured or rushed when bouncing from one appointment to another. If you have ever had a therapy appointment, you are already familiar with the "50 minute hour". Why 50 minutes? The extra 10 minutes gives the therapist time to write progress notes, deal with billing issues, take a short bathroom break, and get ready for their next client.

27. **Give yourself a time "range".**

    Instead of telling your date you will meet them at the restaurant at 5:00 sharp, let them know that you will be there between 5:00 and 5:15. For estimations on what time you will be home from work, especially if you are working late or traffic affects your commute, you can give a broader estimate such as "between 6:00 and 7:00". You can also predict that "dinner will be ready between 6:00 and 6:30." This technique prevents people from pointing at the clock and saying, "A-ha! You're three minutes late!" It prevents you from stressing out and speeding to your destination to avoid being berated for tardiness.

Conclusion

Because time blindness is one of the symptoms that is accompanied by the neurodevelopmental disorder ADHD, it is not well-understood. Since time blindness is the inability to sense the passage of time or accurately measure time, you now understand that it is not an intentional disregard for time, but rather, a sensory issue that can make nearly every aspect of your life more difficult.

You discovered that time blindness affects the past, present, and future. Time blindness affects the past because you will have trouble knowing how long ago something happened, the present because it is difficult for you to judge how long an activity takes, and it affects the future because it makes it difficult to plan.

In Chapter 1, when you learned what time blindness was, you saw that relationship issues are one of many problems that can occur as a result. The people in your life frequently mislabel your time blindness as "poor time management" because they are unaware of what time blindness is. Since the people in your life do not understand the nature of time blindness, they also do not have compassion for when you:
- Lose track of time
- Chronically arrive late
- Miss deadlines

- Feel like time is slipping away
- Overestimate/underestimate how much time has passed
- Do not know how much time remains before an event
- Do not know how long tasks take
- Have difficulty sticking to a schedule
- Find it hard to create realistic schedules

When time blindness shows up as other, albeit more subtle issues, the following can occur:

- Difficulty regulating the speed of movement
- Slow reaction or response time
- Procrastination
- Boredom
- Impulsive behavior
- Inability to get organized
- Misaligned intentions vs actions
- Chronic lateness
- Struggling with last minute assignments
- Being misjudged for being lazy
- Feelings of inadequacy
- Seeing yourself as a disappointment to others
- Difficulty recalling how long ago an event happened

In chapter 2 when you learned how time blindness really feels, you grasped the concept that people with time blindness have consistent challenges with time reproduction (repeating a task for the same amount of time it previously took), time sequencing (correctly recounting the order in which events occurred), and perceiving time (estimating how much time is left before an upcoming event/how much time has elapsed).

In fact, since time blindness feels as if one is suspended in an eternal present, you could set a pot of water to boil, forget to set the timer, and walk away for what seems like "5 minutes", only to come back several hours later to find an empty pot as all the water has evaporated - and a potentially dangerous situation if you find yourself staring at a red-hot pot on the stove!

Many people with time blindness fail to meet deadlines since they have no idea how to plan the project to ensure completion by the deadline. Some suffer greatly for our mistakes. In fact, it's likely that your perception of time is the source of myriad misunderstandings and painful experiences.

In chapter 3 when we looked at a quick 20-minute self-test, you probably realized you do in fact suffer from time blindness. Since the first part of this test involved setting your phone's timer for 10 minutes and seeing how much you could get done around the house, without looking at the timer, you realized how easy it is to misjudge the passage of time.

The second part of this test involved setting your phone's timer for 10 minutes again, but this time playing on your phone for 10 minutes - you remember the difference between the two parts of this test, right? In the first part, although it likely felt rushed, you noticed that you were able to get more accomplished while challenged by a ticking clock that you couldn't see. However, during the second part when you could see the clock, you were probably surprised to see that you were caught off-guard when the timer went off. It is also likely that these 10 minutes seemed to fly by and you lost track of time.

In chapter 4, answering 9 of the most common questions relating to time blindness likely offered you insight, including:

- How time blindness turns your life into extremes
- How to combat time blindness
- Some negative consequences of time blindness
- How to explain time blindness to your loved ones
- Benefits to being time blind
- Whether or not time blindness is only linked to ADHD
- How to stop hyperfocus before it starts
- The types of problems time blindness may cause
- When you should turn to mental health professionals for help

Finally, in chapter 5, the 27 time blindness hacks helped you become aware of time and finally begin to get a handle on how you spend your time, no longer feeling like it's sand slipping through your fingers.

These hacks included:
- Identifying the areas of impact
- Allowing for free time
- Reminding yourself why you are making these changes
- Setting timers
- Consciously tracking time
- Leveraging apps to assist you
- Keeping clocks in every room in the house set to different times
- Getting enough sleep
- Carving out time to plan
- Breaking up daunting tasks
- Setting multiple alarms

After reading this book, you should now understand that time blindness is truly a symptom of ADHD, a genuine mental illness, as opposed to an excuse for being inconsiderate or flaky. Since people with time blindness often disappoint others due to missed deadlines or appointments, this improved understanding of the condition may make it easier for you to educate those in your life so they can better understand and have compassion for those who suffer from this affliction.

Whether you or your loved one has time blindness, you are now able to understand how it feels. Furthermore, the hacks listed in this book will enable you to live your best life by being a master of your time - and no longer being its slave.

Printed in Great Britain
by Amazon